A Light on My Path

*David Durston is Chancellor of
Salisbury Cathedral*

A Light on My Path

*Praying the Psalms
in the Contemporary World*

David Durston

CANTERBURY
PRESS

Norwich

First published in 2002 by the Canterbury Press Norwich (a publishing imprint of Hymns Ancient & Modern Limited, a registered charity)
St Mary's Works, St Mary's Plain
Norwich, Norfolk, NR3 3BH

© David Durston 2002

David Durston has asserted his right under the Copyright, Design and Patents Act, 1988, to be identified as the Author of this Work

British Library Cataloguing in Publication data

A catalogue record for this book is available from the British Library

Unless stated otherwise all quotations are from the Psalter contained in *Common Worship: Services and Prayers for the Church of England* (Church House Publishing, 2000), copyright © The Archbishops' Council, 2000 and are reproduced by permission.

1-85311-4626

Typeset by Regent Typesetting, London, and printed in Great Britain by Creative Print and Design, Wales

*Your word is a lantern to my feet
and a light upon my path.*

(Psalm 119:105)

With many thanks to the musicians, choristers
and choirmen of Salisbury Cathedral whose
delightful singing has added so much to my
enjoyment of the psalms.

Working with the staff of the Grubb Institute of
Behavioural Studies over the years has greatly
extended and deepened my thinking about the
interaction between the realities of human
experience and Christian theology, and I am
grateful to them for that.

Contents

CONTENTS

The God of Abraham praise
Who reigns enthroned above
Ancient of everlasting days,
And God of love;
To him uplift your voice
At whose supreme command
From earth we rise and seek the joys
At his right hand.

Though nature's strength decay,
And earth and hell withstand,
To Canaan's bounds we urge our way
At his command.
The watery deep we pass,
With Jesus in our view,
And through the howling wilderness
Our way pursue.

The goodly land we see,
With peace and plenty blest,
A land of sacred liberty
And endless rest;
There milk and honey flow,
And oil and wine abound,
And trees of life for ever grow
With mercy crowned.

There dwells the Lord our King,
The Lord of Righteousness,
Triumphant o'er the world and sin,
The Prince of Peace:
On Sion's sacred height
His kingdom he maintains,
And glorious with his saints in light
For ever reigns.

The God who reigns on high
The great archangels sing,
And 'Holy, holy, holy' cry
'Almighty King!
Who was, and is the same,
And evermore shall be:
Eternal Father, great I AM,
We worship thee'.

Part One
Introducing the Psalms

> Let the word of Christ dwell in you richly ...
> and with gratitude in your hearts
> sing psalms, hymns and spiritual songs to God.
>
> Colossians 3:16

Why Read the Psalms?

The first Christians sang and prayed the psalms as an essential part of their worship. In this they followed the example of Jesus, and of those who had gone before them in the Jewish faith.

As a young boy and as an adult Jesus worshipped with other members of His community in the synagogue at Nazareth. Here He learned the psalms. Some of them He learned by heart so that He was able to quote them. He prayed the psalms. Through them He learned to pray. When we pray them, we join our prayer with His.

Through the centuries His followers have continued His example. Generations of Christians have read, prayed and sung the psalms, although the ways they have done so have been very varied. Great cathedrals and large monasteries have maintained the tradition of singing the psalms each day in choir. Thousands of Christians, some perhaps very isolated, have read and prayed them each day on their own. Through them the whole Church offers up its prayer and praise to Almighty God, and all who pray them join their prayers to the prayers of Jesus and of the Church.

A major part of the reason why generations of people have continued to pray and sing the psalms is that they speak about experiences that are common to people everywhere.

In the psalms people tell God frankly and directly about how they are feeling. They are sad or worried or frightened or depressed, and they tell God and cry out for help. They are relieved, delighted, overjoyed, and they sing their psalm of thanksgiving and praise to the Lord who has been good to them.

Through the psalms we can speak to God about our own pain and our gratitude. We can also put ourselves alongside other people in their suffering or rejoicing and pray the psalm on their behalf.

The approach of this book is to explore the experience of the psalmists, their pain and their joy, their anguish and their anger, and to see how they related their experience to the Lord they served. This leads into suggestions for praying the psalms from our experience of the world of today.

The psalms teach us how to pray. Dietrich Bonhoeffer, the German theologian and pastor executed for his opposition to the Hitler regime, wrote: 'In the Psalter we learn to pray on the basis of Christ's prayer. The Psalter is the great school of prayer' (*Life Together*, page 37).

> Most of Scripture speaks to us;
> the Psalms speak for us.
>
> Athanasius

What Are the Psalms?

The word 'psalm' is the English version of the Greek word *psalmos* which appears several times in the New Testament, including the quotation at the top of this introduction. This Greek word translates the original Hebrew word *mizmor* which means a song or poem sung to the accompaniment of stringed instruments. It appears in the title of fifty-seven psalms.

One hundred and fifty psalms form part of the Hebrew Bible, the collection of books which Jesus knew as 'the Scriptures'. The psalms were the first and largest book in the third section of the Scriptures. In Hebrew the book is called *tehillim*, which means 'songs of praise'.

How the psalms began

From the earliest times men and women cried out to God for help in times of danger and distress, and shouted out in praise when the danger was averted.

The origins of psalms can be found in these early prayers.

Whether they are cries of pain and fear or shouts of joy, these prayers are a reaction to events and situations. They are spontaneous. This spontaneity in response to circumstances is a characteristic feature of many psalms.

The psalms as we have them emerged at a later stage. They are poetic compositions which take the original spontaneous reaction of anguish or of joy, and express it in a form that can be used by many different people in a worshipping congregation. Where this has been done well the spontaneity is not lost, so that it is clear the psalm originated in the cry of someone in distress, or in a joyous shout of gratitude and praise, and only later came to be used in worship.

When the psalms were written

With some exceptions, it is not possible to date the psalms accurately, partly because many of them show signs of having been revised over the centuries. The earliest go back to the time of King David (c. 1010–970 BCE). Some belong to the period of the first Temple (c. 960–587 BCE) when the people of Judah were ruled by their own king. Many may have originated in this period but were subsequently revised and adapted.

In 587 BCE Jerusalem was attacked by the Babylonian army and captured after a long siege. It was a cataclysmic event in the history of the Jewish people. The whole city, including the Temple, was destroyed. Large numbers of people, including all the leading families, were taken away into exile in Babylon.

After many years of exile they were allowed to return to their homeland by King Cyrus of Persia after he had captured Babylon in 538 BCE. Over the next thirty years many parties returned. They began to rebuild the city of Jerusalem. The Temple was rebuilt between about 520 and 515 BCE.

In the years that followed, those who served in the Temple formed collections of psalms written in earlier years and composed new ones for use in the Temple. Some of those they collected were originally private prayers, and occasionally they added extra verses to adapt them for use in public worship. Some of those they composed were for singing at particular feasts and ceremonies (although now we often do not know what these ceremonies were like). Eventually the psalms were brought together in the collection we now know as the Book of Psalms or the Psalter. So the Psalter has been called 'The Hymn Book of the Second Temple'.

But that is only part of the story. Most people would have heard the psalms and learned to say and sing them in the synagogue. Here the local congregation gathered for learning, praise and prayer. The psalms were an essential part of the worship of the synagogue. The Psalter was the hymn book the congregation learned by heart.

It is probable that nearly all of the psalms were written by men, and collected and edited by men. But the Old Testament includes some very ancient songs that are attributed to women. The best known is the Song of Deborah and Barak in chapter 5 of the Book of Judges. Hannah's Prayer in chapter 2 of the First Book of Samuel is in the form of a psalm. In reading the psalms we need to be open to the possibility that some of them were originally composed by women.

What is important for us in reading and praying the psalms is not when they were written, or how they were used centuries ago. What matters is the spirit that inspired them and shines through them, and the way they are able to help us in our lives and in our relationship with God today.

Where the psalms were written

The heartland of the people who wrote the psalms is in the mountains on the west side of the River

Jordan and the Dead Sea. The western slopes of these mountains receive good rains in winter and spring, but the eastern sides are dry and barren. This contrast is often reflected in the psalms.

On the west side grew grain and figs, vines and olives, and the psalmists sometimes picture the hills clapping and singing with delight. But even in the fertile area the balance was precarious. Many streams which were full of water in winter dried up in summer. If the dry summer season was prolonged and the winter rains were poor, the crops did not grow, and hunger or even starvation threatened.

Some parts of the country, particularly in the north, were heavily forested, and the trees too are pictured as clapping and singing.

In the desert areas to the east only sparse scrub-like vegetation grew, but the shepherd who knew his way around could lead his flock of sheep to find enough to eat if he kept moving them on each day.

The animals of desert and forest often appear in the psalms – lions, deer, wild goats, snakes and birds, as well as farm animals like sheep and oxen.

For much of Israel's history the coastal areas of the Mediterranean were inhabited by people who were traditional enemies of Israel. As a result the Israelites tended to have little contact with the sea, and tended to regard it as threatening and dangerous.

The Hymn Book of Israel

The Book of Psalms

The one hundred and fifty psalms in the Hebrew Bible, together with the rest of the Hebrew Scriptures, were first translated into Greek. This translation was carried out by a team of seventy scholars and so is known as the Septuagint (abbreviated LXX), from the Greek word for 'seventy'. Subsequently they have been translated into hundreds of different languages. They form part of the Old Testament of our Christian Bibles.

The psalms are intended to be sung as much as to be read. For this reason they are included in many books used in corporate worship, among them *Common Worship* and the *Book of Common Prayer*. Because they are printed in these books in the form that is designed for singing, some of the verses are sub-divided so that the numbering of the verses may be slightly different from that in the Bible. This is noted in the comments on each psalm in each book.

When one tries to get an overall view of the Book of Psalms, at first sight it looks a complete jumble. The psalms do not seem to be in any logical order.

However, within the Book of Psalms there are

groups which clearly belong together. For example, psalms 120–134 all have the title 'A Song of Ascents' – in Hebrew, *ma'a lot*. They clearly form a collection designed to be used by pilgrims going up to Jerusalem.

Similarly, psalms 3–41 nearly all have the title 'A Psalm of David' (although we should not assume that means they were actually written by David). They are addressed to 'The Lord' (Hebrew *Yahweh*) rather than to 'God' (Hebrew *Elohim*), and nearly all are personal rather than communal. They form another collection. Psalms 51–72 are another series of Psalms of David addressed to God (*Elohim*).

The Book of Psalms is probably best understood as a collection of smaller collections, into which some individual psalms have been inserted in a rather haphazard way. It is as if the compilers had some psalms for which there was no obvious place, and they simply slipped them in rather as one might slip a single sheet of paper into a loose-leaf folder to keep it safe.

The Jewish scribes divided the Book of Psalms into five books, in imitation of the Five Books of Moses at the start of the Bible. The five books are:

- Book One: Psalms 1–41
- Book Two: Psalms 42–72
- Book Three: Psalms 73–89

- Book Four: Psalms 90–106
- Book Five: Psalms 107–150

Each of the first four books ends with a short doxology, such as

> Blessed be the Lord God of Israel,
>   from everlasting to everlasting. Amen.

The order in which the psalms are placed does not give much clue as to their meaning. Other features provide a clearer guide, particularly the different types of psalms that can be identified.

The weight of this sad time we must obey,
Speak what we feel, not what we ought to say.

William Shakespeare, *King Lear*

The truthfulness of the psalms

The psalms contain some of the most vivid descriptions of human experience ever written. They give us a picture of what people are going through, and what it feels like to go through it.

The range of experience and emotions they describe is very varied. Pain and fear, joy when a disaster is averted, hope and despair, love and trust in God, hatred of enemies and longing for revenge: all these are in the psalms.

The distinctive feature of the psalms is that these are all addressed to God. He is told about them, and no punches are pulled. There is none of that politeness that focuses on the more pleasant and positive feelings, and regards unpleasant and negative feelings as unsuitable for prayer and worship addressed to the Lord.

There is a bluntness and an honesty about the psalms as a whole. They tell it the way it is without glossing over the uncomfortable bits. They are truthful, true to human experience, true in describing what people are going through and telling the Lord what it is like.

> The Psalms – poems which have survived for centuries
> to speak a living word to us today.
>
> Claus Westermann

The psalms as poetry

The psalms are poetry, but they are Hebrew poetry, which is very different from English poetry or that of any other European language. There are very few rhymes in Hebrew poetry. Its sense of metre is not related to syllable, but rather to the balancing of two parts of a verse. This balancing (or parallelism, as it is often called) is a key feature of Hebrew poetry.

In a typical form of this, the second part of a verse does not add a new thought, but repeats or echoes the first. For example:

> The earth is the Lord's and all that fills it,
>> the compass of the world and all who dwell therein.
> For he has founded it upon the seas
>> and set it firm upon the rivers of the deep.

>> (24:1–2)

Another example of this parallelism is

> The heavens are telling the glory of God
>> and the firmament proclaims his handiwork.
> One day pours out its song to another
>> and one night unfolds knowledge to another.

>> (19:1–2)

Sometimes this parallelism takes the form in which the second part is in contrast to the first, perhaps its total opposite:

Some put their trust in chariots and some in
  horses,
    but we will call only on the name of the Lord
    our God.
They are brought down and fallen,
    but we are risen and stand upright.

(20:7)

Recognising this parallelism adds to the pleasure that comes from reading or singing the psalms.

The Hebrew poets also loved playing with words and letters. Much of this is inevitably lost in the translation into English. One aspect worth noting is the alphabetical psalm, where each verse or each line starts with a successive letter of the Hebrew alphabet – often called an acrostic. Psalms 9/10, 25, 34, 37, 111, 112, 119 and 145 are all alphabetical psalms. For example, in psalms 111 and 112 each line starts with a different successive letter of the alphabet. In psalm 25 it is each verse that starts with a successive letter. Psalm 119 is a particular *tour de force* – twenty-two stanzas of eight lines each, each of the eight lines beginning with the same Hebrew letter, and covering the twenty-two letters of the Hebrew alphabet in order.

The titles of the psalms

Many of the psalms in the Hebrew Bible have titles. These are usually printed in English versions of the Bible but are not included in Prayer Books or Psalters.

Some titles would seem to be tunes. It would be nice to know what the delightfully named 'The dove on the far-off terebinths' (psalm 56) actually sounded like. Other titles seem to be the names of the choirs for whom they were originally composed – for example, 'Of the Korahites' or 'A Psalm of Asaph'.

The commonest title is 'Of David'. This does not necessarily mean that David wrote the psalm. It can mean that it is part of a collection of psalms composed or collected and named after him.

Fourteen titles refer to events or situations in David's life. Eight of them are related to the time when David was on the run from King Saul who was trying to capture him and kill him – psalms 7, 34, 52, 54, 56, 57, 59 and 142. Again the titles do not necessarily mean the psalms were written by David at that time. They can mean that as people pondered these very frightening situations that David faced, they responded by composing these psalms. The value of these titles is that they provide us with a way of exploring the meaning of the psalm.

> The Book of Psalms places lament, petition, praise, thanksgiving, doubt and meditation on wisdom side by side in a colourful mixture.
>
> Erich Zenger

Different Types of Psalms

Although they have been loved by many generations of Christians, the psalms are often not easy to understand. At a first reading some of them seem strange, even peculiar. Their difficulty can discourage and put off the reader who is not familiar with them.

In part this is because they are poetry. More significantly, they are Hebrew poetry. They use figures of speech and metaphors that are strange to us. We do not naturally think of a thunderstorm as a way of picturing the glory of God. Psalm 29 does! To appreciate the psalms we need to find a way of entering into the thinking of those who wrote and sang them so that we can experience their meaning.

A vital key to this is to appreciate that there are different types of psalms, and to recognise which type any particular psalm is.

For example, some psalms are prayers for help. Others are songs of thanksgiving for the help that has been given. Others are songs expressing confidence and trust. Some psalms are hymns of praise.

Some psalms arose out of the experience of a single person. Others have come from the experience of a community or of the whole nation of Israel.

By recognising the type of psalm we are reading or singing we can catch its mood and enter into its spirit.

While the different types are distinctive, there is a great variety within each type, and that is part of the attraction of the psalms. The types are not rigid compartments. Some psalms start as one type and end up as a different one. Some seem to have elements of two different types.

Five main types can be identified.

Cries for help

The very simplest form of prayer is the cry of someone who is in trouble or in danger, 'God help me.' This cry to God for help lies at the heart of many of the psalms. They are often known as laments.

Laments are prayers for help that come out of a wide variety of different kinds of situations, from sickness and pain, from being bullied and threatened and oppressed, from danger in war, and from the sense that death is near.

The initial cry for help with which the psalm

opens is often expanded with a description of the speaker's situation. It presents to God how awful the situation is, as a way of urging him to act and to provide a way out of it. This description of the situation is the *lament*, although perhaps *complaint* or *protest* would be more natural terms today. The speaker is complaining to God because of the way God is treating him. He is protesting at what is happening to him. (For the moment we will assume it was a 'he', though it may have been a 'she'.)

Many of the psalms of lament are concerned with the speaker's personal situation, but others are the prayer of the whole community. The nation is facing disaster. The crops have failed and the spectre of famine looms near. Or a powerful enemy is threatening to invade the country and people's lives are in danger.

In some cases disaster has already overwhelmed the country, and the lament is a cry of agony from a people mourning their dead and grieving over the destruction of their homes and their city. Their complaint is that the Lord they trusted has let them down.

But the typical lament does not end with the complaint. The speaker has prayed his prayer. He now trusts that God has heard and will answer it. So he ends his prayer on a note of confidence and thanksgiving.

Laments provide us with prayers that we can pray when life is rough. When we are in constant pain, when we have lost a job and are out of work, when friends have turned against us, when we are being bullied or oppressed, psalms of lament can express what we feel and turn it into a prayer to the Lord.

But laments are prayers we can pray at other times too. When things are going well for us, we read the lament and we are reminded of brothers and sisters in Christ for whom life is hard. We remember friends who are ill, or depressed, or grieving the death of someone they love. We remember Christians who are bullied or discriminated against because of their faith, people who are caught up in violence and war, and those who do not have enough to eat and go to bed hungry night after night. When we read the psalms of lament, we can make them our prayer for these people.

One of the great values of reading the psalms in a regular and systematic way, perhaps following a lectionary, is that they remind us that whatever we are feeling, there are others who are feeling differently. The psalm becomes a way of sharing their experience.

The Seven Psalms

Within the laments are seven psalms which have a distinctive emphasis. In most of the laments the speaker is experiencing pain, isolation or abuse which he feels is undeserved. He is holding the Lord responsible, and calling on Him to take action to relieve his distress.

In the Seven Psalms the speaker is more ready to acknowledge that he has contributed to his unhappy situation. He acknowledges that his own shortcomings are responsible for his trouble. In some there is an explicit confession of sin. In others it is only a hint. These psalms convey a more intimate relationship with the Lord, and an awareness that there is something wrong with this that needs to be put right.

This grouping of seven psalms – 6, 32, 38, 51, 102, 130, 143 – is a long-established tradition in the Church. They are often described as the Seven Penitential Psalms. In the medieval period they had a special place in the Church's liturgy, especially in the Visitation of the Sick and in the Ash Wednesday rites. They were often included in Primers and Books of Hours, collections of prayers for use at home. They were designed to move people to sorrow for their sinfulness.

They profoundly influenced Martin Luther. He

lectured on them in 1512–13, at a time when he was struggling with a crisis of faith. He was deeply moved by their expression of penitence, and the powerful sense of the mercy and forgiveness of God that they convey. Together with his study of the Letter to the Romans, they enabled him to break through to a new understanding of the gospel.

Songs of thanksgiving

Songs of thanksgiving are closely related to laments, in that both of them come out of a situation of distress in which the speaker has cried to God for help. But in the thanksgiving song the speaker is now on the other side of the situation. God has heard the cry for help and has acted in response to the complaint.

The song of thanksgiving tells a story, the story of a rescue from danger or from a painful or disastrous situation. It reports how the speaker was in trouble and how God acted to save him.

Other songs of thanksgiving describe how the whole nation was in danger, under attack, facing the threat of being overwhelmed. Then the Lord acted, and they were rescued.

Here are psalms to read when our faith is shaken and we begin to doubt that God will ever help us out of our present situation. Here are psalms that remind us to give thanks when all seems well.

Songs of trust and confidence

The songs of trust are a development of the lament and the song of thanksgiving. The typical lament includes an expression of trust and confidence that God will hear the prayer addressed to him and answer it. Sometimes this is expanded so that it becomes the main theme of the psalm. There is no urgent cry for help. The dominant note is one of confidence. This is the key feature of a song of trust.

Compared with songs of thanksgiving, songs of trust are more general and less immediate. The speaker is looking back on the experience of God's care and protection over the years, and reflecting on it. The psalm speaks in general terms of a relationship with the Lord that is utterly trustworthy in the face of every threat.

This trust in God springs out of experience of his continuing faithfulness. Knowledge of this experience from which trust has developed needs to be shared with others to encourage them to trust too.

Psalms of trust and confidence are often people's favourite psalms. When they are read in times of anxiety or sadness, they provide reassurance and strengthen faith in God's love and care for his people.

One of them, psalm 23, 'The Lord is my Shepherd', is probably the most widely loved of all the psalms. It has been the inspiration of two wonderful hymns. 'The Lord's my shepherd, I'll not want', from the Scottish metrical Psalter, sung to the tune 'Crimond', is a favourite at both weddings and funerals. George Herbert's hymn, 'The King of love my shepherd is', is also greatly loved.

> The Psalms are the poetry of the reign of the Lord.
>
> James B. Mays

Songs of the Kingdom of God

The faith of the people of Israel at its best was much wider than their own nation. It offered a world-wide vision, embracing all the nations of the earth, and the whole created world.

They worshipped the Lord who had rescued them from slavery in Egypt and led them through the deserts of the Sinai peninsula to their homeland by the River Jordan. He had won a great victory over the powerful Egyptian army. Every year they celebrated their escape from slavery at the Feast of the Passover, the greatest festival of the year.

Some of the psalms are victory songs, telling the story of how the Lord defeated the slave-masters of

Egypt and set his people free. Some look forward to the time when He will defeat the forces of evil throughout the world. He will become 'King of all the earth' (psalm 47:2), establishing His reign of peace and justice over His whole creation.

These songs that celebrate His victory and look forward to His coming reign can best be described as Songs of the Kingdom of God.

Some of these psalms speak of the Lord coming to judge the earth (e.g. psalms 96 and 98). 'To judge' in this context means to intervene on behalf of the poor and the vulnerable, to protect them from the powerful who are oppressing them. This was one of the responsibilities of the King of Israel (see psalm 72:2, 4, 12–14).

These psalms give us a picture of the reign of God. For example, psalm 146 speaks of the Lord

> Who gives justice to those who suffer wrong
>   and bread to those who hunger.
> The Lord looses those who are bound;
>   the Lord opens the eyes of the blind.

(146:6–7 *Common Worship*; 7–8 Bible)

Jesus was familiar with these psalms. Their message of God's future rule, the world-wide peace and justice He will bring, His special care for the weak and the vulnerable, shaped Jesus' teaching about

[25]

the Kingdom of God. These passages in the psalms, and similar ones in the prophets, are the seeds which came to fruition in Jesus' message of the good news of the reign of God.

They look forward to the central theme of the good news that Jesus announced. His message is summarised in St Mark's Gospel: 'The time is fulfilled and the kingdom of God is at hand; repent and believe in the good news' (Mark 1:15). It is this hope that underlies the prayer that Jesus taught us to pray: 'Thy kingdom come ... on earth as it is in heaven' (Matthew 6:10).

These psalms invite us to look at the world around us, its pain and suffering, its violence and brutality, its unfairness and the lack of care and consideration we also often show. They encourage us to pray for the coming of the Kingdom of God into all these situations.

Psalm 47 is a song of God's Kingdom and there is also a collection of them later in the Book of Psalms (Psalms 93, 95–99).

Hymns of praise

The other major type of psalm is the great song or hymn of praise. All the psalms are sometimes regarded as hymns of praise, but the term is probably best used to refer to public songs (as opposed to personal or intimate ones), which are sung praising God for His character and His activity.

They frequently start with a summons to praise, calling people, perhaps calling the natural world, to praise God. They then go on to give the reasons for praising God. They speak of His goodness, His graciousness, His faithfulness, His steadfast love. They also speak of how He forgives and heals and redeems and sets free.

Psalm 103 is perhaps the most familiar of these because of the well-known hymn based on it: H. F. Lyte's 'Praise my soul the King of heaven'.

The last five psalms in the Book of Psalms, 146–150, are all hymns of praise. They are sometimes called 'Hallelujah psalms' because they all begin with the Hebrew word *Hallelujah*, which means 'Praise the Lord'. They are also sometimes referred to as the 'Laudate psalms', because that is the first word of these psalms in Latin.

It seems almost certain that they have been deliberately put at the end of the Psalter because the end of all our praying is praise. Praising God is the supreme expression of all worship and prayer.

Other types

In addition to these main types there are several others that occur less frequently. **Creation songs** describe the beauty and glory of the world as a way of giving praise to the God who created it. Psalm 104 is the clearest example of a creation song. Psalm 8 is probably the best known. The first part of psalm 19 is also a creation song.

The Hebrew word that is translated 'law' in our English Bible is *Torah*. The word 'law' will mislead us if it makes us think in terms of lots of rules and regulations. Torah is the revelation of Himself that a gracious God has made to His people. In it He has shown what He is like – merciful, loving, trustworthy and fair – and has given guidance to them on how they are to live in the world that He has made. **Songs of Torah** express delight and wonder at the way God has revealed Himself and cares for His people. Psalms 1 and 119 are the clearest example of songs of Torah. Psalms 15 and 24 are also songs of Torah, set in the form of songs to be sung in procession to the Temple.

Songs of Zion praise the glory of Zion or Jerusalem as the city of God, the home of the Temple, the dwelling place of God. Psalms 46, 48 and 87 are songs of Zion. Psalms 122 and 132 are pilgrimage songs rejoicing in Jerusalem.

The **Royal Psalms** focus on the King, who is

descended from King David, with whom the Lord has made a special covenant (see, for example, 89:19–37). The King was central to the life of the people of Israel. The key theme in these psalms is the shout, 'The Lord is King'. The King reigning in Jerusalem, the city of God, was seen as the earthly representative of the King who reigns in the heavens. He was also the embodiment of his people. When the King was righteous and just, the people prospered. When the King was evil, the people suffered. Hence the particular significance of the Royal Psalms in the Book of Psalms. Psalms 2, 20, 21, 45, 72, 89, 101, 110 and 144 are Royal Psalms.

There are **psalms of historical recital** in which the story of the nation's history is told in terms of its relationship with the Lord. Psalms 78, 105, 106, 135 and 136 are psalms of historical recital.

Finally there are **wisdom psalms** in which the understanding that has come from years of reflection on the experience of life by generations of those who have studied the Law is set out and sung. In this way it is passed on to the present generation and those who will come after them. Psalms 37, 49 and 112 are clear examples of wisdom psalms.

> In the Psalms we learn to pray on the basis of
> Christ's prayer.
> The Psalter is the great school of prayer.
>
> Dietrich Bonhoeffer

How to Read the Psalms

The psalms were collected together so that they
could be used in worship. They are hymns and
prayers addressed to God. This distinguishes them
from other types of writings in the Bible, such as
history, law, prophecy, gospels and letters.

The Book of Psalms is part of the Bible. Like other
parts of the Bible, Christians regard the psalms as
inspired by God. When we read a passage from one
of the Gospels, or part of one of the letters in the
New Testament, we are aware that God may speak
to us through it. The same is true of the psalms.

It is generally helpful to read the Bible when one
is on one's own, and not likely to be interrupted.
(Put the ansaphone on!) It can also be a help to be
in a place where one can read aloud without worrying about being overheard.

But while these things are helpful, they are not
always practical. Some people who commute to
work by train or bus read the Bible on the way to
work each morning. It may be the only time in

the day when they are on their own and uninterrupted.

While the psalms are part of the Bible, their distinctive feature is that they are addressed to God. They are hymns and prayers we are invited to make our own. We are given words in which we can speak to the Lord. This is a good reason for reading and praying the psalms aloud.

Some of them are intended to be sung by a congregation, like a hymn in a church service. Sometimes a hymn calls on us to 'rejoice' when we do not feel like rejoicing. It invites us to set aside our unhappiness and our dissatisfaction and focus on the goodness of God and the good reasons we have for being thankful. Sometimes the psalms do the same.

Other psalms are very personal. They started as the prayer of a particular person in a particular situation. It may be helpful to read them through quietly first, thinking

- How is this person feeling?
- What is happening to make them feel like that?

The comments on each psalm in this book are often designed to help you work this out. You may then like to think

- Is this how I am feeling?
- Is this what I want to say to God?

- If I do not feel like this, are there other people I know who do?
- Have I heard of people, or can I imagine people, who are in this kind of situation?

It may be that you are called to put yourself in their shoes to pray this psalm with them and for them.

Then you can pray the psalm, reading it aloud. You may like to end with a short prayer of your own, expressing in your own words your response to the psalm.

Difficulties in reading the psalms

There are three common difficulties that people today often experience in reading the psalms.

Are the psalms self-righteous?

The first is the tendency of the psalmists to divide people into two contrasting camps. They speak on the one hand of 'the righteous', 'those who fear the Lord', and on the other hand of 'the wicked', 'sinners'.

They assume that they are among 'the righteous' and those who are against them are 'the wicked'. They fix all the blame for the situation they are in on 'the wicked'.

People today can find this irritating, even offensive. The psalmists can come across as complacent, smug, self-righteous. They seem too pleased with themselves, too quick to condemn others. They 'get up our noses'.

We are also aware of the damage that has been done by religious people who have assumed they are right and those who disagree with them are wrong. We sympathise with Oliver Cromwell's comment, 'I beseech you in the bowels of Christ, believe that you may be mistaken', and we know how difficult he found it to practise this.

If we are to be able to pray these psalms, we need to understand the kind of situations from which they come and the mind-set of those who first prayed them.

Many of these psalms come out of situations in which people are very frightened or have been badly hurt. When people are weak and vulnerable, those threatening them seem very powerful and malevolent. The fear and the pain give rise to wild imaginings. That is why those who are threatening them are sometimes pictured as wild beasts threatening to bite and eat them or trample them to death.

Underlying the psalms as a whole is a keen sense of the critical distinction between those who have set themselves to serve the Lord and live in His way, and those who ignore Him. For the psalmists this is the most important decision in a person's life.

By 'the righteous' they mean those who have committed themselves to living in accord with the way of the Lord. They are truthful and do not tell lies or run people down. They are honest and fair in their dealings and generous in giving freely to those in need. They live in a way that makes for peace and well-being in the community.

When they speak of 'the wicked' or 'sinners' they mean those who are selfish, arrogant, deceitful, violent. They damage the peace and well-being of the community because they ignore the guidelines the Lord has given showing people how to live.

When we are aware of the fear and the pain that lies behind these psalms, and of the way those who first prayed them felt passionately about the importance of serving the Lord, then these psalms feel much less complacent and smug.

Dietrich Bonhoeffer offers another perspective on these 'psalms of innocence' in *Life Together* (page 38). It springs from his emphasis that the psalms are the prayers of Jesus Christ. We pray the psalms as those who are 'in Christ', 'members of Christ', so that we pray them in and with Him.

'Can we, with the psalmist, call ourselves innocent and righteous?' he asks. 'In so far as we are ourselves, we dare not do so.' We are aware of how far we are from being righteous, but we know that Jesus Christ was the one wholly faithful servant of God. One of the key promises of the gospel is that He gives us His righteousness. 'We can pray the psalms of innocence as Christ's prayer for us and gifts to us.'

If you find it difficult to pray or sing these psalms, remember that you are not just speaking for yourself. You are speaking as one who has been given Christ's righteousness.

The nationalism of the psalms

A second difficulty people experience in reading the psalms comes from the way the Christian gospel has widened our understanding of the meaning of 'the people of God'.

In the Old Testament the people of God were a single nation. They had their own King, their own capital city. They believed they had been chosen by God for a special purpose. As a nation certain distinctive features marked them off from other nations: circumcision, observance of the Sabbath, food laws.

In the New Testament the people of God are not a single nation but are drawn from all nations. All are invited to become disciples of Jesus Christ,

God's own people, regardless of nationality or ethnic origin. The boundary markers such as circumcision have been abolished. (The first really big row
in the Christian Church was over the question: Do
the Gentiles have to be circumcised like the Jews
in order to become Christians? The apostle Paul
fought against this requirement, and by winning
this battle (see Acts 15) he ensured that the
Christian Church was not simply a Jewish sect but
became an open and ultimately world-wide community of faith.)

The awareness of being specially chosen by God
sometimes led the people of Israel to feel they were
superior to other nations. Because they were a
small nation surrounded by larger, sometimes
aggressive, neighbours, from time to time they had
to defend themselves against attacks and invasion.
This gave rise to an aggressive, militaristic kind of
nationalism which is very far from the Christian
spirit.

It sometimes emerges in the psalms. Psalm 149 is
an example, with its sudden switch from the praise
of God to the defeat and imprisonment of enemy
nations:

Let the faithful exult in glory;
    Let them sing for joy on their couches.
Let the high praises of God be in their throats

and two-edged swords in their hands,
to execute vengeance on the nations
and punishment on the peoples,
to bind their kings with fetters
and their nobles with chains of iron.

(Psalm 149:5–8 NRSV)

Fear of foreigners, and in particular the fear of being absorbed by an alien culture and losing their own identity, sometimes caused the people of Israel to be very exclusive in their attitudes. In the Book of Ezra, the insistence that Israelites who had married foreign wives during exile in Babylon should divorce them is a terrible example.

Other parts of the Old Testament are written in a very different spirit and emphasise that Israel has been called by God for the sake of all nations. The blessing of Abraham – 'in you all the families of the earth shall be blessed' (Genesis 12:3) – the Books of Ruth and Jonah, the poetry of the second part of Isaiah, all emphasise that 'the Holy One of Israel' is 'the God of the whole earth' (Isaiah 54:5).

The nationalistic parts of the psalms, particularly those that are aggressively nationalistic, are very difficult for Christians. Perhaps we should read them, ponder them, but recognise that as they stand we cannot make them our prayer.

> The Psalms of enmity and vengeance
> are a cry for justice and righteousness.
>
> Erich Zenger

Cries for justice: cries for retribution

In some psalms those who pray them ask that their enemies may be punished, humiliated, injured or even killed. In places there is a violence which can be deeply offensive. Some of the language used is horrendous.

They present an acute problem for Christians. We remember the teaching of Jesus and the spirit in which He calls all His followers to live:

> You have heard that it was said, 'You shall love your neighbour and hate your enemy.' But I say to you, 'Love your enemies and pray for those who persecute you.'
>
> (Matthew 5:43–44)

This is the spirit in which we, as followers of Christ, are called to respond to those who hate us and take advantage of us and make life hard for us.

The psalms which pray for the punishment of enemies seem totally contradictory to the spirit of Jesus Christ, but there they are, bound up in the same book with some of the most profoundly spiritual writing in the world. How are we to make sense of them?

It is very easy to dismiss these parts of the psalms as pre-Christian and anti-Christian, and simply ignore them and leave them out. But if we do this we fail to understand them and lose the opportunity to learn from them. We need to struggle with these 'vindictive psalms' (as they are often called) if we are to learn from them about our relationship with God.

Victims of war crimes

The first thing to recognise is that these psalms come from people who have suffered terribly. They have been the victims of what we would now call 'war crimes'. They have been through the same kind of things as people in Bosnia or Kosovo or the Sudan. They have had their children kidnapped or murdered, their loved ones tortured or raped. It is very hard for those for whom life has gone well to understand their terrible pain and suffering.

They are now powerless – prisoners of war, perhaps, or exiles in a refugee camp. Every day they are struggling with overwhelming feelings of hopelessness and despair. They are inclined to give up faith in God, to feel that He has abandoned and deserted them or is powerless to help them. In this situation to cling to the Lord and to cry to Him is a source of hope. It offers strength to hold on to one's human worth in the face of a situation that dehumanises.

Their appeal to 'the Judge of all the earth'

In their powerlessness they cry to the Lord for justice. He is 'the Judge of all the earth'. They call on Him to act as judge, and to intervene in the situation to put right the terrible injustices they have suffered and are continuing to suffer. It is the appeal for justice which underlies these psalms.

Events of recent years have shown that the families of people who have been murdered or killed in tragic circumstances feel a deep need to see those responsible for their deaths identified. The families of the victims of the Lockerbie air crash are a well-known example of this. Some have dedicated years of their lives to searching for those responsible. They have been unable to find rest or peace until these people have been tried and convicted. Those who prayed the psalms expressed a similar spirit. Unable to take any action themselves, they cried to the Lord to judge and convict those responsible.

The kind of justice they are calling for is retributive justice. To use a modern parallel, it is like the compensation or damages that someone is required to pay to a victim whom he has injured or whose property he has stolen or damaged. It is an appeal that says, 'Do to them what they have done to us.'

Retributive justice

They are cries for retribution rather than revenge. To take revenge is to act in retaliation for the injuries one has suffered. But those who prayed these psalms did not seek to take revenge. They did not, probably could not, take action, but they handed the situation over to the Lord, asking Him to take the action and leaving it to Him. He is trusted to take what action is appropriate, but in His own way and in His own time, and not necessarily in the way the speaker would have chosen. The language is sometimes plaintive, sometimes vicious, but it is always addressed to the Lord, calling on Him to take action.

The perspective of the psalms is consistent with that of St Paul when he writes:

> Beloved, never avenge yourselves, but leave room for the wrath of God; for it is written, 'Vengeance is mine, I will repay, says the Lord.'

(Romans 12:19, quoting Deuteronomy 32:35)

Acknowledging anger and hatred

It is also important to recognise the psychological and spiritual insight of these psalms. They are honest and truthful in acknowledging and expressing the anger and the rage that people feel. They do not deny unpleasant, 'bad' feelings. They are not caught up in a false spirituality that keeps God and negative feelings apart.

Those who have been victims of criminal brutality often experience an intense burning rage arising out of all they suffered. This rage needs to find expression. Modern psychological insight has taught us that to repress anger and rage does not eliminate aggression and violence, but allows it to fester, hidden and out of sight.

Unrecognised anger may smoulder and find expression in other ways. It can eat away at a person's heart so that they become bitter and vindictive.

The other alternative is that the anger is expressed but it is not submitted to the Lord. Then it may lead to acts of revenge and violence that may injure and destroy other people.

Pastors and counsellors know that pain and hate is not restricted to those whose suffering is public and visible. There is the pain of those who feel their parents never loved them as they loved their brothers and sisters. There is the pain of those who were humiliated by influential adults when they were children. This pain can give rise to a deep anger and hate, but such anger and hate is often buried.

Anger, hatred and fear have to be acknowledged and expressed before release from them can be found. They become manageable when they are brought to consciousness. These psalms put this anger and fear into words. They dare to express what is really felt, and so offer a way of dealing with it. Sometimes they are like a scream that can awaken unsuspected feeling.

But anger and hatred are not the end. Acknowledging and expressing them is the way of being released from them. In the psalm the anger and hate are acknowledged and expressed, expressed with passion and intense feeling, but they are brought into the presence of God and submitted to Him.

We may choose not to say these parts of the psalms. But we may also choose to say them on behalf of those who have suffered terribly, to an extent we can hardly imagine, and who have to live with a burning anger towards those who have caused them so much suffering and pain.

Jesus Christ, who suffered for his enemies

Dietrich Bonhoeffer adds a further dimension to our understanding of the cursing psalms (*Life Together*, pages 34–40; *The Psalms: Prayer Book of the Bible*, pages 21–23). It is based on his emphasis that the psalms are the prayer of Jesus Christ: 'Jesus Christ prays through the psalms in His congregation … Those who pray the psalms are joining in with the prayer of Jesus Christ.' He also writes: 'Christ prayed on the cross for His enemies and taught us to do the same. How can we go on calling down God's vengeance on our enemies as these psalms do?'

He points out that the enemies referred to are the enemies of God's cause. This is not a personal quarrel. At no point do the psalmists plan to take vengeance into their hands. They entrust that entirely to God. Their prayer is that God's justice will be carried out in the judgement of sin.

But Jesus Christ took the sinners' place and suffered the judgement for which these psalms pray. He took the judgement on Himself and so He forgave His enemies. He suffered so that His enemies might go free.

Bonhoeffer comments: 'So the cursing psalm leads to the cross of Christ, and to God's forgiving love of His enemies'. 'As members of Jesus Christ, we can pray these psalms through Jesus Christ.'

Bonhoeffer's profound spiritual and theological insight enables us to find Christian meaning in these parts of the psalms which are in some ways so alien from the spirit of Jesus Christ.

Some will conclude that they cannot say these parts of the psalms. It is wise that they are excluded from public worship where people of different outlooks and levels of understanding come together to pray.

Other people, hesitantly and aware of their own sinfulness, will decide to say them, on behalf of those who have to live with the intense rage that comes from having suffered terrible violence, always remembering that Jesus Christ took this judgement on Himself.

A final comment

When you read the psalms, always remember that you are praying the psalms with many other people and for many other people. From time to time, and especially when the mood of the psalm does not fit your own mood at all, stop and ask yourself: For whom am I praying this psalm?

Remember that the psalms are the prayers of Jesus Christ. When you pray them, you pray them with Him, as one who is 'in Christ'.

Glossary of Key Names and Terms

Aaron. The brother of Moses and high priest. The phrases 'house of Aaron' or 'sons of Aaron' mean 'the priests'.

Abraham. The founding father from whom the people of Israel traced their descent. He was honoured as a man of great faith, who at the call of God set out without knowing where God was ultimately leading him. His story is told in Genesis 12–25. His name means 'ancestor of a multitude'.

Alleluia. See 'Hallelujah' below.

Asaph. A musician and hymn-writer from the tribe of Levi, after whom a choir was named. See the heading to psalms 50 and 73–83 in most Bibles.

Covenant. One of the key ideas of both Old and New Testaments, it describes a solemn and binding agreement between two parties, setting out the responsibilities and privileges of each. In the Bible there are frequent references to the covenant between the Lord and His people. The Lord makes a covenant with Abraham (Genesis 15 and 17), which has a strong emphasis on the promises made to Abraham. There is the covenant made at Sinai through Moses, after the people of Israel had escaped from Egypt, which included the giving of the Law or Torah (Exodus 19 – 24). There is also a covenant made with David, which is central to Psalm 89. These are all aspects of the Old Covenant or Old Testament. (The two English words are both translations of the same Greek word.) Jesus Christ brings a New Covenant or New Testament. It is referred to in His words at the Last Supper, usually read at every Eucharist or Holy Communion, when He says, 'This is my blood of the new covenant which is shed for you and for many for the forgiveness of sins.'

David. The shepherd boy from Bethlehem who became King of Israel around 1000 BCE. Later generations looked back to him as the ideal King. Psalm 89:9–37 tells the story of the promise made to him. He played the harp and composed and sang songs, and centuries later the Jewish scribes attributed many of the psalms to him.

Enemies. There are many references in the psalms to 'enemies' but it is not often specified who they are. Israel was a small nation living in the midst of larger and more powerful nations that were often hostile to it. Some of the enemies are national enemies, i.e. armies of foreign nations attacking or threatening Israel. Sometimes they are members of other nations or ethnic groups among whom Jews were living. Sometimes they are personal enemies, powerful people who are bullying or making life hard for the psalmist.

Ephraim. One of the sons of Joseph, and later one of the tribes of Israel. After the division of the kingdom (see 'Kingdom' below), the capital of the northern kingdom was Samaria which was situated in the territory of Ephraim. Ephraim is sometimes used to mean the northern kingdom of Israel.

Exile. When Jerusalem was first besieged by the Babylonian army in 597 BCE, the King surrendered. He, most of the royal family, royal officials and leading citizens, several thousand people in all, were deported into exile in Babylon. Many of the treasures of the Temple were looted and taken to Babylon. A puppet King was installed. Eleven years later, following a rebellion, Jerusalem was again attacked by the Babylonians. After a long siege the city was overrun in 586 BCE, and a large number of people were again deported. The Temple, the royal palace, and the large houses were all burned to the ground and the city walls broken down. Until then most Israelites had believed the Temple could never be destroyed because it was the Temple of the Lord, and He would protect it. Its destruction, and the experience of exile, forced them to rethink their faith. The Book of Isaiah, chapters 40–55, and the Book of Ezekiel are the two major writings of this period. In 538 BCE the Persian army under King Cyrus captured Babylon. He allowed exiles to return to their homelands. Over the next forty years several groups of Jews returned to Jerusalem and began to rebuild the city.

Exodus. The escape of the Israelites from Egypt, where they had been forced to work on the grandiose building projects of the Pharaohs (or kings) of Egypt. The Israelites saw this escape and the events around it as the work of the Lord. There are numerous references in the psalms as to how He delivered them from slavery in Egypt. This escape, and the years of travelling in the wilderness that followed it, gave the people of Israel their identity as a nation.

Hallelujah. A Hebrew word which combines hallel, meaning 'praise', and Jah, an abbreviation for 'the Lord' – hence 'Praise the Lord'. It is sometimes written 'Alleluia'.

Israel. The name both of a person and of a people. Jacob (see below) was given the name Israel, which means 'one who has wrestled with God and prevailed' (or possibly) 'God who strives and prevails'. The story of how he received this name is told in

Genesis 32. His descendants took his name so that the word 'Israel' is often used in the Old Testament to mean 'the people of Israel', 'the Israelites'.

Jacob. The son of Isaac and the grandson of Abraham, he was given the name Israel (see above). He was the father of twelve sons. The twelve tribes of Israel were named after these sons. The name Jacob is sometimes used to mean 'the people of Israel'.

Jerusalem. The capital city founded by King David. The name means 'foundation of peace'. For the destruction of the city, see 'Exile' above.

Jews. The name 'Jew' came into use after the exile in place of the earlier name 'Israel' or 'Israelite'. It is derived from Judah or Judea, the area around Jerusalem. Judah was one of the sons of Jacob and one of the tribes of Israel.

Joseph. One of the twelve sons of Jacob (see above). His name and story are well-known through the musical *Joseph and the Amazing Technicolour Dreamcoat*. His story is told in Genesis chapters 37 and 39 – 50. The name Joseph is sometimes used for 'the people of Israel'.

Judah. One of the sons of Jacob and one of the tribes of Israel. Its territory was in the south in the area around Jerusalem. Following a rebellion after the death of Solomon, the kingdom divided, and the southern kingdom, with its capital Jerusalem, was known as Judah. (See 'Kingdom' below.)

Kingdom. Saul was the first King of Israel, but it was his successor David (see above) who established the Kingdom. He later came to be regarded as the ideal King. After the death of David's son, Solomon, the Kingdom was split by a rebellion. The northern kingdom, Israel, with its capital Samaria, survived until it was overwhelmed by the Assyrian army in 721. The southern kingdom, Judah, with its capital Jerusalem, was ruled over by descendants of David until it was destroyed by the Babylonian army in 587 BCE. (Within the nation some believed that the monarchy as an institution was a fundamental mistake, because the Lord was the only King of Israel and no human being should be given that title.) The failure of kings to live up to people's hopes, and later the destruction of the city of Jerusalem and the subordination of the Jews to other nations, led them to look for an ideal King. He would be sent by God, would be like David and would liberate them from foreign powers and re-establish their independence as a nation.

Kingdom of God. See the section 'Songs of the Kingdom of God' (page 24).

Korah. The Korahites were a group of Levites (i.e. from the tribe of Levi) who served as singers and musicians in the Temple choir, and as doorkeepers and caretakers. See the headings to psalms 42–49 in most Bibles.

Law. The English word usually used to translate the Hebrew word *torah*, though *torah* has a wider meaning – see *Torah* on page 54.

Lord. 'The Lord' (printed in capitals in the Bible) is used to translate the Hebrew name for God, *YHWH*, which is usually pronounced *Yahweh*. It is sometimes abbreviated to *Yah*, as in *hallelujah* (see above). The story of the disclosure of this name comes in Exodus 3 (Moses at the burning bush).

Mercy. Often translated 'steadfast love' in modern translations, the Hebrew word *chesed* or 'mercy' describes the faithful love and loyalty that binds partners in a covenant (see above). It is God's faithfulness to the covenant He has made with Israel, despite Israel's failure to keep that covenant.

Moses. The leader of the people of Israel in the Exodus from Egypt (see above).

Peace. A comprehensive word which means more than just absence of war or peace of mind. It describes the whole well-being of the community and the person, physical, mental, spiritual, social, economic, political. So to pray for the peace of Jerusalem (psalm 122) is to pray for the welfare of the city and all who live in it or visit it.

Pit. Used as an alternative to 'Sheol' to describe the place of the dead (see 'Sheol' below).

Righteous. An important word in the psalms, and one we often find difficult to understand today. We hear it as meaning 'self-righteous' – that is to say, smug, pleased with themselves, thinking they are good. The psalms speak about those who have committed themselves to living in accord with the way of the Lord. Several psalms describe them (e.g. 15, 24, 112). They are truthful and do not tell lies or run people down. They are honest and fair in their dealings. They are generous both in giving freely to those in need and in lending to others. They live in a way that makes for peace (see above) and well-being in the community and throughout the world. These are the sort of people the psalms call 'the righteous'.

Salvation. In the psalms to be saved is to emerge safely from a dangerous situation, such as illness, battle, or slavery. Salvation means to be healed, to be freed, to be victorious. It is always the work of the Lord God. The supreme act of salvation is the Lord's saving His people from slavery in Egypt at the Exodus (see above). The Hebrew word for salvation, *yeshuah*, is the basis of several names including 'Joshua' and, when turned into Greek, 'Jesus'.

Sheol. The place of the dead. When the psalms were written, before people had any hope of resurrection from the dead, those who had died were thought to have a shadowy existence in an underworld called Sheol or the Pit.

Sinai. The mountain between the Gulf of Suez or the Red Sea and the Gulf of Akaba. The Israelites went there during the journey through the wilderness. It was there the covenant between God and the people of Israel was made and the Ten Commandments were given. It is also called Horeb in the Old Testament. Its modern name is Jebel Musa.

Torah. Usually translated 'law', its meaning is wider than that. It can mean 'teaching' or be used to describe the Lord's revelation of Himself as a reliable and generous God – see Psalm 19. 7–10. People thought of it as the Maker's instructions for living in the world He has made. Jews felt, and still feel, a great affection for the Torah. It is sweeter than honey and more desirable than gold (verse 10).

Victory. The Hebrew words *yasha*, *yeshuah* and *teshuah* can be translated 'salvation', 'deliverance', 'safety' or 'victory'. When you are in a battle facing an enemy who is determined to defeat you and probably kill you, the only way to be saved is to win the battle and defeat him. Whether it is Israel facing its enemies in battle, or the Lord God facing all the forces of evil opposing Him, salvation means victory over these enemies.

Wicked. Used in the psalms as the opposite of 'the righteous' (see above). It describes people who are selfish, arrogant, deceitful, violent. Psalm 10:1–11 is a typical picture of them. They damage the peace and well-being of the community because they ignore the guidelines the Lord has given showing people how to live.

Zion (or Sion). Another name for Jerusalem (see above).

Key Themes in the Psalms

This index is designed to assist in choosing psalms to read, pray and sing on particular occasions or to address particular concerns. It offers a selection of psalms on a wide range of themes, but it is not a complete index of all the themes in the psalms. *Please note:* The numbers are the numbers of psalms, not page numbers.

Psalms for the Christian year

Advent 25, 80
Christmas 8, 96, 98
Lent 6, 22, 38, 51, 102, 130, 143
Good Friday 22 especially, also 69, 88, 130, 143
Easter 114 especially, also 105, 113, 117, 118
Ascension Day 8, 47, 93, 110
Pentecost (Whitsun) 33, 104, 145 and 139:1–18

Further Reading

The book that I have found most helpful in reading the psalms is Walter Brueggemann's *The Message of the Psalms: A Theological Commentary* (Augsberg Publishing, Minneapolis, 1984). In this book he combines a deep understanding of the Hebrew text and a capacity to relate the psalms to the experience of life today. His social and psychological insight make this an exceptionally valuable book. I found it quite hard work but very stimulating and enlightening.

A very useful commentary that covers all 150 psalms in James L. Mays' *Psalms* in the series *Interpretation: a Bible Commentary for Preaching and Teaching* (John Knox Press, Louisville 1994). The great strength of this book is its emphasis on the theme 'the Lord is King' as the central theme of the psalms, that the psalms are 'the poetry of the reign of the Lord' (page 30). In seven pages (29–36) he provides a fine succinct summary of the theology of the psalms.

I have also valued Claus Westermann's *The Living Psalms* (English translation: T. & T. Clark, Edinburgh 1989) and John Goldingay's *Praying the Psalms* (Grove Books, Nottingham 1993).

The book that helped me most in making sense

of the vindictive psalms was Erich Zenger's *A God of Vengeance?* (English translation: Westminster John Knox Press, Louisville, 1996) – a demanding book to read, but worth the effort.

Jonathan Magonet gives a Jewish view of the psalms in *A Rabbi Reads the Psalms* (SCM Press, London 1994). His deep feel for the Hebrew language often produces quite unexpected insights and helped me to understand how the psalmists used Hebrew poetical forms to express their meaning.

Dietrich Bonhoeffer, the German theologian who was executed by the Nazis, offers many perceptive insights into the use of the psalms as a resource to help and nourish our prayer. They can be found in *Life Together* (English translation: SCM Press, London, 1954) in the section 'The Secret of the Psalter', and also in a small book, *The Psalms: Prayer Book of the Bible*, a translation published by the Sisters of the Love of God, Convent of the Incarnation, Fairacres, Oxford OX4 1TB.

A Suggested Daily Reading Plan

A Suggested Daily Reading Plan

	Month A	B	C	D	E	F
1	1	27	53	77	119:113–120	125
2	2	119:25–32	54	78:1–31	101	126
3	3	28	55	78:32–55	102	119:145–152
4	4	29	56	78:56–72	103	127
5	5	30	119:57–64	79	104:1–23	128
6	6	31	57	80	104:24–35	129
7	7	32	58	119:89–96	105:1–22	130
8	119:1–8	33	59	81	105:23–45	131
9	8	34	60	82	119:121–128	132
10	9	119:33–40	61	83	106:1–23	133
11	10	35	62	84	106:24–47	119:153–160
12	11	36	63	85	107:1–22	134
13	12	37:1–20	119:65–72	86	107:23–43	135
14	13	37:21–40	64	87	108	136
15	14	38	65	119:97–104	109	137

16	119:9–16	39	66	88	110	138
17	15	40	67	89:1–18	119:129–136	139
18	16	119:41–48	68:1–20	89:19–51	111	140
19	17	41	68:21–35	90	112	119:161–168
20	18:1–30	42 & 43	119:73–80	91	113	141
21	18:31–50	44	69:1–18	92	114	142
22	19	45	69:19–36	93	115	143
23	20	46	70	119:105–112	116 & 117	144
24	119:17–24	47	71	94	118	145
25	21	48	72	95	119:137–144	146
26	22	119:49–56	73	96	120	147
27	23	49	74	97	121	119:169–176
28	24	50	75	98	122	148
29	25	51	119:81–88	99	123	149
30	26	52	76	100	124	150

In those months which have 31 days, read Psalm 146 on the 31st day. In February read two psalms on the 27th and two on the 28th.

Please note: The numbering of the verses here follows the numbers in the Bible. In a few of the psalms the numbers in *Common Worship* are slightly different, as some verses are subdivided.

Part Two
A Commentary on the Psalms
and Suggestions for Prayer

> The human heart is like a ship on a stormy sea
> driven by winds blowing from all four corners
> of heaven ...
> Such storms teach us to open our hearts ...
> The Book of Psalms is full of heartfelt words
> made during storms of this kind.
>
> Martin Luther

Book One
Psalms 1 – 41

Psalm 1
The blessings on those who follow the
Lord's guidance

Their delight is in the law of the Lord.

This psalm is an introduction to the whole Psalter, and sets out its central theme. The people of God are called to live their whole lives in a way that accords to the Lord's purpose, and so fulfils His intentions for the world He has made. The fundamental contrast in life is between those whose lives are in line with God's intentions set out in His Torah (revelation or law, verse 2; refer to the paragraph on *Torah* in the Introduction, p. 61), and those who ignore them. Those who live in tune

with the guidance that Torah gives will be nour-
ished and refreshed like a tree by the side of a
stream and their lives will be fruitful (the first half
of the psalm), but those who ignore it are headed
for disaster (the second half of the psalm).

- Picture in your mind a line of fruit trees alongside
  a river. Their leaves are fresh and green and their
  branches are weighed down by all the fruit they
  are carrying. Hold this picture in your mind, and
  think of a number of people who are important
  to you. Pray for yourself and for them, that you
  may all live in such a way that you are fruitful
  like these trees.

Psalm 2
A royal psalm, celebrating the Lord's protection of the King

You are my son; this day have I begotten you.

This is a royal psalm, the psalm of a nation which
sees its life as a community focused on its King. If
the King is successful the whole nation prospers. If
the King fails, the whole nation suffers, just as the
death of King Harold at the Battle of Hastings in
1066 sealed the defeat of the English army.

Now the nations surrounding Israel plot against the Lord and his King (verses 1–3). But the Lord has promised his King that he will rule over them (verses 4–9). The psalm is an expression of confidence in the Lord's power to protect the King whom He has enthroned (verse 6). The rebellious rulers are warned that they would be wise to submit (verses 10–end).

'Anointed' (verse 2), in Hebrew *Messiah*, was one of the titles of the King of Israel. When the monarchy came to an end with the capture and destruction of Jerusalem, the title was given to the hoped-for ideal King of the future. It is translated in Greek as *Christos* and became the title given to Jesus when He was recognised as the promised Messiah.

In verse 7 the Lord addresses the King: 'You are my son'. As Christians we are used to thinking of ourselves as sons and daughters of God. This is the result of the way Jesus taught us to address God as 'our Father' and His emphasis on the Fatherhood of God in His teaching. In the Old Testament the Lord is only thought of as Father very occasionally. But the King was seen as having a special relationship with the Lord. He was the Lord's representative, reigning in Jerusalem, the city of God. So it was natural to regard him as a son of God.

• Keep silence for a few minutes and hold in your mind the idea of Christ as King over all the nations of the earth, bringing in His rule of peace and justice. Then think of a country where peace and justice are clearly lacking, and pray for that country that peace and justice may spread throughout it.

Psalm 3
A cry for protection and an expression of quiet confidence

But you, Lord, are a shield about me.

The Hebrew title suggests that this psalm has its origins at a time when King David's hold on the throne of Israel was threatened by a rebellion led by his son Absalom. David was forced to leave Jerusalem and flee into the hills. Many people abandoned David, believing that his cause was lost, and went over to Absalom. They were saying in effect and perhaps saying publicly, 'The Lord is no longer going to help David' (see verse 2). The story is told in 2 Samuel 15 and 19.

In the face of this frightening situation, while this psalm is primarily a prayer for protection against personal enemies, it is marked by a strong sense of confidence and trust. The description of the psalm-ist's situation is quite brief, only two verses (verses I–2), and moves into an expression of trust in the Lord's protection (verses 3–6).

The prayer at the end (verses 7–8) has a violent streak in it (verse 7). Note that the psalmist is not asking the Lord to do this. It is a statement about God's judgement. He will act in power to silence those who, by what they say, are undermining His good purposes. Perhaps there is also the recogni-tion that Absalom was not the sort of person who would ever negotiate, so that his rebellion could only be ended by force.

• Reflect on whether there are people you feel are hostile to you or are acting in a way that makes things difficult or painful for you. Think of others who are in this situation, either people you know or people you have heard or read about. Pray that you and they may be delivered from this oppressive situation. Express your confidence that the Lord is like a shield around you.

Psalm 4
A prayer for fair treatment and a song of trust

*Commune with your own heart upon your bed,
and be still.*

This psalm is a prayer from someone who is being dishonoured and disgraced by people who are talking about her (verse 2). It begins as a prayer for fair treatment, calling on God as a God of 'my right' or 'my righteousness' (verse 1), but then becomes an expression of trust and confidence.

The speaker begins by calling on God to listen and answer. She remembers a previous experience when she was released at a time of distress (verse 1). She then appeals to her enemies – an unusual feature seldom found in the psalms. She asks them to consider what they are doing, to pause and change, and put their trust in the Lord (verses 2–5). She ends the psalm with a personal statement of what it means to her to trust in the Lord (verses 7–8).

- Be still and put yourself in the position of those addressed in the psalm. Are there people who find you difficult or oppressive? Are there people who have been disadvantaged or have suffered as a result of decisions or actions you have taken?

Are there people, perhaps in other parts of the country or other parts of the world, who feel that the group you belong to, or your country, have neglected them and abandoned them?

Psalm 5
A prayer for guidance in the face of lies and deception

Lead me, Lord, in your righteousness,
because of my enemies;
make your way straight before my face.

A prayer for guidance in a situation where all around people tell lies and are deceitful. The psalm starts by calling on the Lord and making clear that the speaker has something he wants Him to hear (verses 1, 3). It emphasises to the Lord that He is a righteous God who hates lies and deceitfulness. Only then does the speaker come to the heart of his complaint. People are lying and deceitful, totally dishonest. He thinks they are trying to deceive him and lead him astray, so his prayer is that the Lord will make his way straight. The psalm ends on a note of confidence in the Lord's protection.

- Are there situations where you find it very difficult to know what is the right thing to do, and where there are factors that may mislead you or distort your judgement? Do you know other people in that kind of situation? Pray for yourself and them, using the prayer from this psalm quoted above.

Psalm 6
The cry of someone who is acutely ill

Have mercy on me, Lord, for I am weak;
Lord, hear me, for my bones are racked.

The writer of psalm 6 is in pain, unable to sleep at nights, conscious of his weakness, and suspecting that death is not far away. Out of his suffering he cries out to God for healing.

The first part of the psalm (verses 1–5) is his plea. He comes straight to the heart of the problem. He is suffering because the Lord is angry with him. That is the root of the problem. He begs the Lord to change and be gracious to him.

Unlike some other psalms, he does not protest that he is innocent or suggest that the Lord is being unfair in treating him like this. (If you want to make a comparison, look at psalm 17 where the speaker vigorously protests his innocence.) This silence is a tacit admission that his suffering may be deserved, that he has brought his trouble on himself. But there is no explicit confession of guilt, no request for forgiveness. His plea is that the Lord will 'turn' and save his life. He prays for healing in body ('bones') and soul.

The ground of the plea is his desperate condition, his anguish ('sorely troubled') and the nearness of death. The abrupt cry, 'How long?' expresses the pain that lies behind the prayer.

Then in verse 5 he introduces a new argument to stir the Lord to action. If he dies he will no longer be able to praise God. This suggests the psalm was written at a time when those who prayed it had no hope of a relationship with God beyond death. While our understanding has been transformed by the hope of eternal life given to us by the resurrection of Jesus Christ, we can see the force of this argument to those who lived and prayed at a time when there was no such hope.

Verses 6 and 7 are the heart of the complaint. Night after night he lies awake. His pain is such that it reduces him to tears. He is wasting away as a result of his illness, and his spirit is weakened because of those who are hostile to him.

Then in verse 8 there is a complete change of mood. The closing verses of the psalm are a cry of confidence. His cry of pain has been heard by the

Lord. His prayer has been accepted. Those who hate him can go away in shame.

This is the first of the Seven Penitential Psalms (see page 21 of the Introduction).

- Think of people who are acutely ill, in considerable pain, and feeling deeply depressed because they do not seem to be getting any better. There may be someone you know in this situation. Imagine how they are feeling. Hold them in your mind, and pray for them.

Psalm 7
The prayer of someone who is wrongly accused

Let the malice of the wicked come to an end,
but establish the righteous;
for you test the mind and heart, O righteous
God.

This psalm comes from someone who is being unjustly accused, and is deeply hurt by these accusations. He feels that they are tearing him apart (verse 2) and pleads with the Lord to save him.

The references to the Lord gathering an assembly, taking His seat and acting as judge (verses 6–8) suggest that the psalmist may be facing a false accusation in court. He is looking to a higher court and appealing to the judgement of God.

After the opening cry for help (1–2) he protests his innocence of these charges (3–5). He prays to the Lord to intervene (6–9) and expresses his confidence in God as a righteous judge (10–16). In the final verse he promises to give the Lord the thanks he owes.

• Pray for all those who are facing false accusations, especially where those accusations spring from malice or from the desire of powerful and unscrupulous people to further their own interests. Pray for those facing charges in countries where courts are influenced by such factors as racial or religious prejudice or pressure from influential people.

Psalm 8
A song of creation, celebrating the dominion
the Lord has given to humankind

*What are mortals, that you should be mindful
of them?
mere human beings, that you should seek them
out?*

This beautiful hymn, reflecting on the nature of
being human, is chosen both for Christmas Day
and for Ascension Day. We read it on the day when
we celebrate the birth of Jesus, when 'the Word
became flesh and dwelt among us', as John's
Gospel puts it (1:14). We read it again on the day
when we celebrate that the man Christ Jesus
ascended to the right hand of God.

The psalm begins and ends with the praise of God
(verses 1 and 9 in the Bible, 1 and 10 in *Common
Worship*). The sentence 'O Lord our Governor,
how glorious is your name in all the earth', which
opens and closes the psalm, establishes the boundaries within which the rest of the psalm is set.

This central part celebrates humankind as the
focus of God's creation (verses 3–8 in the Bible, 4–9
in *Common Worship*). Its theme is the royalty of
humankind, who have authority and power to
order and care for the world which the Lord has

made (verses 6–8 in the Bible, 7–9 in *Common Worship*). This celebration of humanity takes place within the context set by the Lord's governorship.

The boundaries (i.e. praise of God) and the centre (i.e. affirmation of human power and authority) must be taken together. 'Doxology gives dominion its context and legitimacy' (Walter Brueggemann).

• Reflect on the increased power over creation that science and technology have given, and give thanks for it. Then think of ways in which it has been misused (e.g. the pollution of water and air), and confess to the Lord that we have misused the power that we have been given.

Psalm 9
A song of thanksgiving which turns into a prayer for deliverance

I will give thanks to you, Lord, with my whole heart;
I will tell of all your wondrous works.

Psalms 9 and 10 form a single psalm in the Septuagint, the Greek translation of the Old Testament. They form an alphabetic acrostic, every second verse beginning with a successive letter of the Hebrew alphabet.

The psalm starts on a note of thanksgiving (verses 1–2), an expression of confidence based on what the Lord has done in the past (3–12). Then comes a prayer to the Lord to look and act, followed by a renewed expression of confidence. The last two verses are again a prayer to the Lord to act.

The psalm moves between personal prayer – 'my enemies turned back', 'be gracious to me' – and corporate or national prayer – 'you have rebuked the nations', 'let the nations be judged.'

- Give thanks for a danger averted, a threat overcome, and give thanks for those who work amongst the poorest of the world's poor who struggle with the burden of heavy debts and very few resources.

Psalm 10
A cry of protest at the behaviour of the powerful

They lie in wait, like a lion in his den;
they lie in wait to seize the poor;
they seize the poor when they get them into
their net.

This psalm comes out of a terrible and terrifying situation where those who are poor and vulnerable are at the mercy of powerful and ruthless people who use physical violence and murder to achieve what they want. The description in verses 2–11 echoes some of the worst atrocities committed by military dictatorships and terrorist groups. In response this psalm is a cry of protest to the Lord, and an urgent plea to Him to do something about it.

It also arises out of a struggle over a loss of confidence in the Lord. Terrible things are happening, but the Lord is doing nothing about it. The psalmist calls on Him to explain Himself (verse 1).

The psalmist then gives a long description of what is happening, confronting the Lord with what the situation is really like (2–11) to bring home to Him the need for Him to act (12).

Then comes an indication of a change in mood. 'But you do see!' – the New Revised Standard translation catches this change in mood. Confidence is returning. The Lord is aware of what is happening. The psalm ends on a note of confidence. The Lord reigns and He will act (16–end).

• Where do you think there are situations like that described in this psalm? In a South American dictatorship? A former Soviet republic? A Middle Eastern state? Or in the poorer parts of the larger cities in this country? Think of one or two specific places you know something about and in a prayer describe this situation to the Lord and pray that He will give justice to those who are oppressed.

Psalm 11
A song of trust in the Lord in the face of danger

*When the foundations are destroyed,
what can the righteous do?*

The person who first prayed this prayer was in a difficult situation. People, friends perhaps, were encouraging him to get out of the situation and escape. The nature of the situation is not clear, but it is clearly a dangerous one in which the very foundations of life are being undermined and destroyed (verse 3).

In the face of their warnings and advice, he looks up to heaven where the Lord reigns (verse 4). He expresses his confidence that the Lord is watching the situation. He is righteous and will defeat those who are threatening.

• Pray for Christians who are in situations where 'the foundations are being destroyed' and are struggling with the temptation to pull out – in situations of physical danger where there is war, rebellion or anarchy, or where there is widespread corruption, dishonesty or abuse of power.

Psalm 12
A prayer from a situation where no one can be trusted

*Help me, Lord, for no one godly is left;
the faithful have vanished from the whole
human race.*

This psalm springs out of a situation where hypocrisy is widespread and truth has gone out of the window. It begins with a cry for help from someone who feels that nobody can be relied on (verse 1–4). Then follows a declaration, a word from the Lord, that because the vulnerability of the poor is being exploited, He will act (5–6). In this response to this word of the Lord comes an expression of confidence and a prayer to the Lord that His promise will be carried out.

- Think of those who have been betrayed or let down so badly that they have completely lost faith in other people and feel that no one can be trusted. Pray that they may find a faith in God as One who is dependable.

Psalm 13
The cry of someone in pain and anguish of heart

How long will you forget me, O Lord; forever?
How long will you hide your face from me?

The psalm starts with four questions addressed to the Lord: 'How long ...? How long ...?' They describe the situation and hold the Lord responsible for it. He has forgotten. He is not there when He is needed. The crisis in the relationship with the Lord underlies the pain and distress that is experienced. The speech is terse, as though the pain is so acute that there is no time for polite conversation.

Then comes the request, the plea to the Lord to take action. It consists of three imperatives: '*Consider ... answer ... give light*', followed by three arguments. If God does not act the speaker will die. His enemy will triumph. His foes will rejoice. The language makes it clear that the problem is the Lord's problem. Because the Lord's servant is humiliated, the Lord Himself is diminished.

Then comes the change in mood. It is character-istic of laments but is particularly sharp and notice-able in psalm 13. Something has clearly happened between the painful prayer of verses 1–4 and the trustful confidence of verses 5–6.

The change is introduced by the word 'But' at the start of verse 5. It marks the step forward. The three requests and the three arguments are matched by three expressions of trust: '*I ... my heart ... I*'. Each of these speaks of the Lord: '*Your steadfast love ... your salvation ... the Lord*'. The psalm ends with the 'Because' clause. The change in mood has come because the Lord has responded.

• Think of those whose physical pain or sorrow of heart is so great that it dominates their lives and pushes out almost everything else. Pray that they may be able to take their pain and their sorrow to the Lord in prayer.

Psalm 14
A lament over the folly and wickedness of this age

Everyone has turned back; all alike have become corrupt;
there is none that does good; no, not one.

The psalmist starts by grieving over the folly and corruption of society. It is a deeply depressing picture of a society rotten with corruption and oppression (verses 1–4). There follows a confident assertion that the Lord will take action to overthrow the oppressors and those engaging in corrupt practices (5–7). The psalm ends with a prayer that yearns for the Lord to act. (This psalm is almost identical to psalm 53.)

• Think of those things that give you a sense of despair about society – for example, the widespread use of drugs and the activities of drugpushers, the extent of assaults, rapes and other violent crimes, the casual way some people abandon wives, husbands or partners of many years. Bring them into the presence of God.

Psalm 15
A song of Torah, sung on entering the Temple

Lord, who may dwell in your tabernacle?
Who may rest upon your holy hill?

From one point of view this psalm is a song of Torah. It describes the characteristic behaviour of someone who lives in the way set out in the Torah (or revelation) of the Lord.

At another level it may well have been a liturgy said or sung on entering the Temple. First the question is asked: who is to be allowed to enter? Then the answer is given. What is required is not a special gift or some kind of ritual, but a life lived doing what is right.

The psalm echoes the thought of the eighth-century prophet Micah:

What does the Lord require of you
    but to do justice, and to love kindness,
    and to walk humbly with your God?

(Micah 6:8)

To us today this idea is so familiar as to seem obvious, but in the world of the Eastern Mediterranean when this was written it was surprising, even revolutionary. Religion was then widely seen as concerned with the correct performance of rituals. Morality and the way you lived your life was quite another matter.

• Pray for the Church, that through its worship the lives of its members may be challenged, purified and enriched.

Psalm 16
A song of trust and confidence in the Lord

*You will show me the path of life,
in your presence is the fullness of joy
and in your right hand are pleasures for
evermore.*

The psalm opens with a short prayer for protection, which quickly leads into an expression of devotion to the Lord – and a refusal to be led astray into the worship of other gods. In the second half the psalmist expresses a sense of being blessed, of security and delight.

The last two verses convey the hope of a relationship with the Lord beyond death. The final verse is often used in funeral services.

- Remember the hope we have been given through the resurrection of Jesus Christ from the dead. Pray for those who have been told they have a fatal illness and do not have long to live, those who love them and are close to them in these last weeks, and those who are mourning the death of someone they love.

Psalm 17
A cry for vindication
from someone who believes he is innocent

Hear my just cause, O Lord; consider my complaint.

This is a cry from someone who is being falsely accused. He is surrounded by enemies who are trying to destroy him (verses 9–13). The language is poetic and it is not clear whether they are trying to ruin his reputation, win a judgement against him in a court of law or physically arrest and kill him.

In face of this danger he cries out to the Lord to hear his case, to believe that he is speaking the truth and to vindicate him (1–2). He invites the Lord to try him and examine him and to see his innocence (3–5). At the heart of his prayer is an appeal for justice.

He then appeals to God's steadfast love (6–8). He calls on the Lord to confront those who are attacking him and to rescue him (13–14). He ends his prayer on a note of confidence and hope.

- Pray for those who have been wrongly accused and punished, whether they have been sacked from work, found guilty by a court and convicted, or blamed and held responsible by other people.

Psalm 18
The King's song of thanksgiving for survival and victory

He brought me out into a place of liberty;
he rescued me because he delighted in me.

The Hebrew title of this song of thanksgiving (which is printed in most Bibles) suggests it has its origins in a thanksgiving by King David. It reminds us of the long period that David spent on the run, hiding in the hills and in caves from King Saul and his soldiers who were trying to find him and kill him. The account of this can be found in 1 Samuel 19 – 31. Perhaps the psalm is based on a song composed and sung by David. Awareness of this background helps us to appreciate the joyful, grateful exuberance of the psalm. It is also found in 2 Samuel 22. It divides easily into two parts.

Verses 1–30

The psalm opens with an expression of praise (1–2). The psalmist then describes his situation in metaphorical terms and his cry for help (3–6). The Lord's intervention is then portrayed using the visual imagery of a thunderstorm (7–19). His action is seen as a reward for faithfulness (21–29 *Common Worship*; 20–28 Bible). The section ends with an exuberant expression of confidence in what can be achieved with God's help.

- Think of a situation that might have been disastrous, but which has been transformed, and thank God for it. For example, thank God that the oppressive apartheid regime in South Africa has been brought to an end, and this happened without a destructive civil war and huge loss of life, even though people have been killed.

Verses 31–end

This section tells the story of the battle and the victory. (Most translations put these verses in the past tense so that they describe the battle, but some, including *Common Worship*, put them in a future tense so that they become an expression of trust.) The psalm ends with a hymn of praise and thanksgiving to the one who gives victory to his anointed King (47–51 *Common Worship*; 46–50 Bible).

• Thank God again for a situation which has been transformed, and remember those who have suffered in the process – those who have been wounded, perhaps maimed, those who mourn the death of people they loved.

Psalm 19
A creation song and a song of Torah

The law of the Lord is perfect, reviving the soul.

This psalm links together the themes of God as Creator and the Lord as the Giver of the Law. This link seemed a natural one to Old Testament writers, even if it does not seem natural to us today. The Law of the Lord was His guidance for the world He had made, the maker's instruction book designed to enable people to use it and enjoy it to the full.

It is a psalm in three parts. The first section which speaks of the vast expanse of the heavens, and the last section which speaks of the inner life of the human heart, are not unusual in form. But the middle section, in praise of the Torah of the Lord (see the Introduction, page 28), is very ordered and regular, its six lines using six different synonyms for the Torah, each line describing what it is and what it does. The poem, by its structure, implies that it is the Torah of the Lord, at the centre of life, that gives order and meaning both to the outer world of the heavens and the inner world of the human heart.

In the first section the glory of God is seen in the sky and especially in the sun (verses 1–6). Days and nights are pictured as a choir ceaselessly singing God's praises, though they cannot be heard by human ears (2–4).

In the middle section the psalmist speaks of the glory of the Torah of the Lord, its perfection and its spiritual power. It is a joy and a delight, a treasure more desirable than gold, and nourishment sweeter than honey (10).

In the final section the psalmist allows us a glimpse of the impact the Torah has on him. These precious, delicious words make him want to live in the way that they describe and commend, and so he prays to be protected from both accidental and deliberate breaking of the Law (12–14).

- Pray for yourself and for those close to you that you may find a joy and delight in walking in the way of the Lord, a joy that is sweeter than honey, even though it may at times be costly and contrary to your own inclinations.

Psalm 20
A royal psalm, praying for the King

O Lord, save the king.

The first part of the psalm is a prayer for the King, designed perhaps to be used when a sacrifice is being offered (verse 3). The second part (6–8) is an expression of confidence that the Lord will help. Verse 7 suggests it was used in time of war, before an impending battle.

- Pray for all those who are called on to fight, for example those in the UN or other peace-keeping forces protecting civilians against aggressive militias.

Psalm 21
A royal psalm – a psalm of thanksgiving

You have given him his heart's desire;
and have not denied him the request of his lips.

Clearly designed for public worship, this psalm follows on naturally from psalm 20. It starts full of praise and thanksgiving to the Lord for having answered the King's prayer (verses 1–7). There follows a pronouncement, addressed to the King, and made perhaps by a priest, promising him continuing victory (8–12). The psalm ends with a shout of praise.

• Remembering that the King is the representative of the whole nation, give thanks to God for the many ways in which He has blessed your nation over the years and continues to do so today.

Psalm 22
A cry of anguish from someone facing death

My God, my God, why have you forsaken me?

The opening words of psalm 22 are familiar because they are the words that Jesus said on the cross in His cry of dereliction (Mark 15:34). It would seem that this psalm gave expression to His feelings as He faced death. It is a psalm full of pain, anguish, suffering and fear of being destroyed, but it also has a strong note of confidence and trust. It is the cry of someone in great pain who still wants to assert his faith in God.

It begins with an anguished cry for help, a passionate questioning of God who seems so distant, so unwilling to answer the plea of his suffering servant (verses 1–2). But this triggers the memory of God's faithfulness over the centuries, how He has shown Himself to be one who hears and rescues His people (3–5).

This pattern, of a cry of pain followed by a remembering of God's grace in the past, is repeated. There is a vivid description of humiliation, of facing the taunts of people who are full of hatred (6–8), and then the memory of the God who has proved trustworthy from earliest childhood (9–10). The speaker is holding on to his previous experience as a basis for trust.

This is a psalm marked by sharp changes in mood as two strong feelings are in conflict. There is the feeling of darkness, despair and abandonment, and there is the sense that God is faithful. For a moment one is on top; the next moment the other is stronger.

The cry for help is repeated (11), and the agony of the present situation is spelled out (12–18), followed by a prayer for deliverance (19–21). While the psalmist's pain is vividly described, there is no expression of bitterness or resentment towards the enemies who are maltreating him. The suffering is patiently borne.

Then the mood changes to one of confidence and trust. The Lord will answer. The speaker promises to praise Him, and calls on others to join him in this praise (22–26). The closing verses are a short hymn in which this praise spreads out to the ends of the earth (space) and to generations yet to be born (time) (27–31).

In the accounts of Jesus' death in the Gospels there are several quotations from or allusions to this psalm: the scornful taunts of passers by (7–8), the dividing up of Jesus' clothes (18), the piercing of His hands and feet by the nails (16). It is quite naturally a psalm that is said or sung on Good Friday.

In doing so we are invited to join with Jesus in pressing insistently on God the question as to why He allows so many people to suffer so much. With Jesus we confront God with the pain and anguish we, and many others, are suffering, not holding back out of politeness. But we do this in the context of an underlying confidence, based on

God's faithfulness to His people over the centuries and our own experience of His love and protection in our lives.

- Give thanks that Jesus entered the darkness and despair of dying on the cross, with all its pain and shame and disgrace. Pray for those who are experiencing darkness and despair now, that they may know the presence of Jesus with them now.

Psalm 23
A song of trust in the Lord's provision

The Lord is my shepherd;
therefore can I lack nothing.

Perhaps the best loved of all the psalms, psalm 23 is very widely known through the two hymns based on it, 'The King of love my Shepherd is' by H. W. Baker and 'The Lord's my Shepherd' from the Scottish Psalter. Sung to the tune 'Crimond', the latter is a favourite at both weddings and funerals.

The psalm pictures the Lord as shepherd, guiding, protecting and providing for His sheep as they travel through the wilderness of Judah in search of grass and plants to eat. It anticipates Jesus' picture of Himself as the Good Shepherd in John's Gospel, chapter 10. In verses 4 and 5 the person changes. It is no longer the third person, 'He', a statement or description, but the more intimate second person, 'You'.

The repeated use of the first person, 'I', 'my', might seem to be obsessive in other contexts, but here it is an expression of gratitude and confidence.

• Picture the dry, deserted wilderness, mostly rock and parched earth, with a little scrub-like vegetation, and the shepherd leading his sheep through it, finding the grass that is available, the places where there is water, putting oil on their wounds. Thank the Lord for His care for you.

Psalm 24
A song of Torah, sung in procession

'Who shall ascend the hill of the Lord?'
'Those who have clean hands and a pure heart.'

Psalm 24 is basically a song of Torah (see page 28 in the Introduction), but is in the form of an order of service for a procession, possibly a procession bringing the ark into the Temple. It starts with a short hymn of praise declaring that the Lord is the Creator. Then comes the entrance song (verses 3–6), establishing the sanctity of the Temple as not just a matter of ritual but related to a person's attitude of heart and outward behaviour. Then comes the entrance of the procession with the ark, and two parts of the choirs sing question and answer in response to each other.

• Pray for clean hands and a pure heart, for yourself, for those who are near to you, for all God's people.

Psalm 25
A cry for deliverance from personal enemies

*For your name's sake, O Lord,
be merciful to my sin for it is great.*

This psalm has an interesting and complex structure. It is an alphabetic acrostic, each verse starting with a successive letter of the Hebrew alphabet.

It expresses faith and trust in the Lord, but within it are hints of a painful and threatening situation. The psalmist asks that he may not be ashamed and humiliated (verses 2–3). He asks the Lord to be aware of the violent hatred he is facing (18 *Common Worship*; 19 Bible). He is conscious of his own failures and shortcomings, and of the sense of guilt he feels about them. Twice he asks to be forgiven (10, 17 *Common Worship*; 11, 18 Bible).

Jonathan Magonet, in his book *A Rabbi Reads the Psalms*, suggests it is a concentric psalm, as the following outline shows, with the repeated words in italics (following the Bible's verse divisions):

1–3: The psalmist *waits*: Do not let me be *ashamed*, nor let my *enemies* triumph.

    4–7: Prayers and pleas addressed to the Lord.

        8–10: The character of the Lord, who has made *covenant* with us.

           11: The key verse, 'Forgive me.'

        12–14: The character of the Lord, who has made *covenant* with us.

    15–18: Prayers and pleas to the Lord, expressing the psalmist's personal anguish.

19–21: The psalmist *waits*: Do not let me be *ashamed*, nor let my *enemies* triumph.

Magonet suggests that this very formal structure contains, and partly conceals, an acute personal crisis. The psalmist is in agony of mind, crying out for forgiveness, pleading with the Lord for relief.

The devout prayers of verses 4 and 5 give way to the anguished cry of verses 16–18.

- Pray for those who are troubled in heart, feeling profoundly guilty (whether this is because of what they have done or because they are temperamentally prone to feeling guilty), feeling isolated and lonely in a world that seems hostile and threatening.

Psalm 26
The cry of an injured innocent

Test me, O Lord, and try me.

If the writer of this psalm seems to you at times rather smug and self-righteous, please read the section on page 32–35 in the Introduction. Think of someone who is honestly trying to serve the Lord wholeheartedly and feels very hurt because he (or she) is being wrongly accused. He is open enough to ask God to test him and try him (verse 2).

- Pray for those who are honestly trying to serve God and are bewildered and hurt by what is happening to them.

Psalm 27
A song of trust and a cry for help

The Lord is my light and my salvation;
whom then shall I fear?

In many psalms a cry for help ends with an expression of trust and confidence in the Lord. Psalm 27 is unusual in that it begins with a song of trust and then turns into a cry for help.

The opening verse is a delightful expression of confidence, which is developed through the first half of the psalm. Then in verse 7 (verse 9 in *Common Worship*), the tone changes to one of prayer for help. The psalmist is seeking God's face, pleading with Him not to hide it. (Modern psychological studies have emphasised the importance for the development of babies that they are able to see the faces of their parents. Here the psalmist expresses this intuitively in speaking about seeking the face of the Lord.)

Only towards the very end of the psalm does the painfulness and danger of the speaker's situation become clear. But the psalm ends in the last two verses on a note of confidence.

- Ponder the first verse, printed above these comments. Reflect on fears you have overcome through trust in the Lord, times when you have experienced His light. Express your confidence in Him.

Psalm 28
A prayer for justice and for vindication

My heart dances for joy.

The psalm starts with a cry for vindication. The speaker wants justice. Let malicious people get their just deserts. Then in the middle of the psalm, the tone changes with the words, 'Blessed be the Lord.' He has heard the prayer. The psalm becomes a song of trust and confidence.

• Pray for people who have a deep feeling that they have not received justice, that the Lord has not treated them fairly. Pray that they may be able to express this feeling to the Lord, and find a new and deeper relationship with Him.

Psalm 29
A hymn praising the power of the Lord

The God of glory thunders.

The psalm opens by calling on people to give the Lord the honour and worship that is due to Him (verses 1–2). It then describes His power revealed in the thunderstorm. The thunder is His voice. The hurricane force wind makes the trees thrash about so that whole mountains, Lebanon and Sirion (or Hermon), look as though they are skipping (6). Branches are broken off, the forest stripped bare of leaves.

Then in the last two verses the Lord Himself is pictured sitting majestic and serene above the storm, enthroned as King, giving His people peace.

• Pray for those whose lives are turbulent, who feel they are being blown about all over the place. Pray that amid the turmoil they are experiencing they may know the peace that the Lord gives.

Psalm 30
A song of thanksgiving
for recovery from a life-threatening illness

*You have turned my mourning into dancing;
you have put off my sackcloth and girded me
with gladness.*

The psalmist starts by praising the Lord for rescuing her and healing her when death was threatening (verses 1–3). (Let us assume this time it was she who first sang this.) The whole congregation is invited to join in this thanksgiving and praise (4–5).

Then she tells the story of what happened to her (6–12). Before she was ill she felt perfectly secure. As she looks back, perhaps she feels she was complacent, taking things for granted, not recognising her dependence on the Lord. When she was ill, she turned to the Lord in her distress and appealed to Him. The thrust of her argument was: What good was she to Him if she was dead? The Lord answered her prayer, and turned her pain and anguish to gladness.

- Join your thanks and praise to the psalmist's, for any recovery you made from a serious illness, and for anyone else you know who has made a good recovery. Thank the Lord for the immense advances that have been made in medicine over the past century by which so many lives have been saved and so many people enabled to enjoy good health again.

Psalm 31
Two cries for help

My times are in your hand, O Lord.

This psalm is made of two parts, each of which might be a separate psalm. The first (verses 1–8) begins with a cry for help, a plea for protection and guidance in a situation where the speaker feels there are people trying to trap her (1–4). This cry is followed by an expression of confidence in which the speaker entrusts herself into God's hands (5–6). It ends with a glad acknowledgement of God's help (7–8).

The second part (9–24) also starts with a cry for help. This leads into an agonising description of the speaker's situation. She is sick at heart and full of grief. Physically her strength is ebbing away. Her friends and neighbours have abandoned her and avoid her. She feels people are plotting against her, anticipating that she is soon going to die. Perhaps they have designs on her land and property! She expresses her trust in the Lord again and prays that she will be vindicated. The psalm ends by declaring the Lord's goodness to all who trust in Him.

- Pray for those who feel isolated and lonely, abandoned by friends who no longer care for them or have turned against them.

Psalm 32
A song of thanksgiving for forgiveness

I said, 'I will confess my transgressions to the Lord',
and you forgave the guilt of my sin.

The psalm opens with a general statement, a conclusion reached from reflection on experience: For a full and happy life there is nothing like being forgiven (verses 1–2).

Then the speaker tells his story. Guilt he was not prepared to admit was making him ill (3). Emotionally and spiritually he was dry and withered (3–4).

Then comes the turning point in the story: he acknowledged his sin (5), 'I confessed: you forgave'. The effect for him was like being rescued from a flood, like being given somewhere to hide from the dangers outside. This story, which the speaker tells in the first person, describing his own experience, is a most powerful testimony to the liberating and healing power of forgiveness. Everything depends on confessing. The spoken admission is the way to the release of forgiveness.

The rest of the psalm returns to the teaching style of the opening verses. In the first two verses the Lord is the speaker. The psalm ends by calling on the true in heart to rejoice.

Not surprisingly, in view of its awareness of guilt, this is one of the Seven Psalms (see page 21).

- Pray for those for whom the burden of guilt is heavy, stifling them, paralysing them. Pray that they may confess to the Lord, and experience the freedom and healing that comes from forgiveness.

Psalm 33
A hymn of praise to the Lord,
the Creator and the Ruler of history

He loves righteousness and justice.

The psalm opens by calling on people to rejoice in the Lord and sing His praises (verses 1–3). The reason for this praise is His faithfulness, His righteousness, His steadfast love (4–5). He created the heavens and the earth (6–9). He rules over the destinies of nations, watching over them (13–15), frustrating their plans when He decides (10–11). The psalm ends with an expression of confidence and joy (18–22).

Although the word 'King' is not used, this is 'a new song' describing the Kingdom of God, like psalms 96 and 98.

• Think of those places where powerful rulers use their power to oppress their own people or to threaten or attack other nations. Pray that the Lord may restrain and frustrate this misuse of power.

Psalm 34
A song of thanksgiving
leading into the teaching of wisdom

*This poor soul cried, and the Lord heard me
and saved me from all my troubles.*

This psalm is in two parts. The first part is a song of
thanksgiving. The psalmist begins with a hymn of
praise (verses 1–3). He then gives the grounds for
praise. He was in trouble and he prayed and the
Lord rescued him (4–6). No details are given. The
important point is that he prayed and the Lord
answered. Then he hurries on to urge his hearers to
trust the Lord and see how gracious He is.

This leads into the second part which is in the
style of a teacher of wisdom. The psalmist is trying
to persuade his hearers to trust the Lord and walk
in His way. He sets out conclusions drawn from
long experience. Those who trust in the Lord and
follow His guidance will not be let down. They may
often find themselves in difficulty, but the Lord
cares for the broken-hearted and the crushed in
spirit (18), and they will find He rescues them.

This psalm was the inspiration for the lovely
hymn 'Through all the changing scenes of life' by
Nahum Tate and Nicholas Brady.

- Pray for organisations working with those who are broken-hearted and crushed in spirit. Pray that their staff may have the skill, the patience and the love needed for this task, that they may be agents of the Lord in healing.

Psalm 35
Three cries for help and for justice

Give me justice, O Lord my God.

This psalm consists of three passionate pleas for justice and for protection from enemies. In the first (verses 1–10), the speaker is so frightened and so angry he says hardly anything about his own situation (verse 7 only). After his cry for a shield to protect him from those who are pursuing him (1–3), he launches into a cry for revenge (4–8). (For an understanding of this from a Christian point of view, see the section 'Cries for justice; cries for retribution' on pages 38–45 in the Introduction.) The first cry ends by looking forward to the prayer being answered (9–10).

In the second cry (11–18), he tells the story of what is happening to him. The sense of betrayal and hurt is palpable. His description of his suffering is intended to move the Lord to take action quickly. 'O Lord, how long will you look on?'

In the third cry he re-emphasises the treachery of those ranged against him. They are deceitful liars. He launches into a series of petitions calling on the Lord for justice, arguing that it would be totally unjust for his enemies to triumph over him. Those who are enjoying seeing him in trouble should be made to be ashamed. The psalm ends with an expression of confidence that he will be able to praise the Lord for His fair treatment.

• Pray for those who have a deep sense that life has not treated them fairly, that other people have taken advantage of them, exploited them or betrayed them.

Psalm 36
A prayer for protection
from those who want to cause trouble

He plots mischief as he lies upon his bed.

In some ways psalm 36 is unusual. It starts off with a vivid description of what the wicked are like. Those who reject God's guidance and commands find evil attractive in the depths of their heart (verse 1). They do not expect to be caught (2) and spend a lot of time thinking about what they can do and cause trouble or take advantage of people (4).

Then follows a short hymn, praising the Lord for His love, His faithfulness and His righteousness (5–9).

These first two sections lead into the final section, a prayer for protection from these people (10–12). The way these people think and act, and how evil it is, has been described. The Lord's love and righteousness has been declared. They have been set out to show Him He has a responsibility to act to protect His servants from such people (11). Ultimately they will be defeated (12).

- All around the world there are people whose lives are made a misery by those who take advantage of them – malicious neighbours, greedy landlords or moneylenders, bullying employers, powerful ethnic groups. If you can, recall stories of how such people suffer. Pray for them.

Psalm 37
A wisdom psalm, encouraging trust in the Lord in the face of the injustices of the world

Fret not because of evildoers;
be not jealous of those who do wrong.

As this is a fairly long psalm, you may prefer to read it in
two parts, verses 1–20 and 21–41.

Resentment and envy at the success and happiness
of those who do not deserve them is a very common
human emotion. This psalm is addressed to those
whose faith may be undermined by the injustices
that are so apparent all around them.

It is an alphabetical acrostic psalm. Every second
verse begins with a different successive letter of the
Hebrew alphabet (see page 15 in Part One). By
choosing this regular and orderly structure the
psalmist seems to be implying that the world is regular and in order, in spite of all the appearances of
unfairness. The need to fit this structure may
explain why the psalm tends to repeat itself.

The heart of its argument is in verse 10: the cer-
tainty of retribution for the wicked. This is the
basis of its repeated call to trust in the Lord and
wait for Him, and not fret over things, or become
bitter and resentful.

The second part of the psalm (from verse 21)

focuses on God's continuing protection on those who are guided by Him.

• Pray for those who get upset and whose confidence in the Lord drains away when they see lies believed, and truth ignored, or when selfish and ruthless people achieve their ends through force.

Psalm 38
The cry of someone who is very ill and in great pain

There is no health in my flesh because of your indignation,
there is no peace in my bones because of my sin.

The psalm opens with a cry for help (verses 1–2), but quickly there is an acknowledgement that the problem is not just sickness, but sinfulness (3–4). The belief that illness was a punishment for sin was common in Old Testament times. Jesus challenged and rejected the idea there is any automatic connection between them (e.g. Luke 13:1–4; John 9:1–3). What is often true is that illness or some kind of personal shock or setback makes people aware of their own failings or sinfulness, which they overlooked when things were going well. Here the speaker is ready to acknowledge and confess sinfulness. This psalm is appropriately one of the Seven Penitential Psalms (see page 21 in Part One).

This leads into a long and painful description of the psalmist's situation (verses 5–12). The physical symptoms are agonising, and abandonment by friends and family are felt particularly keenly (11).

Then comes an expression of trust (13–16), quickly followed by a personal confession of sin (18). But the pain of the situation comes back (19–20), and the psalm ends with a renewed cry for help.

This is a psalm that is full of pain. The psalmist seems to have no energy to plead any arguments to spur the Lord to respond except the pain of suffering.

- Bring into your mind someone who is very ill and in constant pain, in hospital perhaps, or in a country where no medical treatment is available and there are no pain-killers. Pray for such people using the prayer in the last two verses of this psalm.

Psalm 39
A cry from someone who is burning with resentment

I held my tongue and said nothing;
my distress increased, my heart grew hot within
me.

Here is a psalm by someone who did not want to complain, but found that as long as she kept silent she was simply burning with indignation. It begins with a vivid description of the psalmist's experience which acts as an argument and an appeal to the Lord. Perhaps she had not said anything because she did not want to encourage those who are sceptical about God. Perhaps she thought she ought not to make complaints to the Lord. But inside she is so angry and resentful that she has to speak.

The second part of the psalm describes her outburst, and then continues with a prayer for forgiveness and for physical healing.

• Pray for those who are outwardly patient and restrained but are inwardly seething with anger and resentment – anger that may be so deeply buried that they do not recognise it is there.

Psalm 40
A song of thanksgiving and a prayer for help

He has put a new song in my mouth,
a song of praise to our God.

This psalm is in two distinct halves. The first part (verses 1–10 in the Bible, 1–11 in *Common Worship*) is a song of thanksgiving for deliverance from trouble. The trouble is vividly pictured as like being trapped in a pit (verse 2), but no specific description of it is given. If we imagine ourselves caught like this in an isolated area, slowly sinking into the bog at the bottom of a pit, we shall feel the sense of terror and rising panic the psalmist felt. He then fulfils the vow made when he was in this desperate situation, not by offering a formal sacrifice or making a thanksgiving offering, but by publicly proclaiming what the Lord has done.

The second part (11–17 in the Bible, 12–19 in *Common Worship*) is a prayer for help. The situation is portrayed as very serious. No details are given, but the person praying this psalm feels overwhelmed by all the hostility and opposition he faces. There are people who are seeking to hurt him or even kill him. The cry for help in the last five verses (very similar to psalm 70) is urgent, but it ends on a note of confidence.

[123]

- Has something happened for which you are very grateful to God? Try to think of something. Then work out whom you should tell about it, so that you do not hide God's love from them. Pray for them, and ponder how you will tell them.

Psalm 41
The prayer of a sick man
for protection from malice and deceit

Blessed are those who consider the poor and needy.

Though it is a prayer for healing in sickness, this psalm starts, not with a cry for help, but with a statement of faith: the Lord blesses those who care for the poor and vulnerable (verses 1–3). Then, perhaps in response to this, comes an awareness and acknowledgement of falling short (4). This leads to a description of the psalmist's painful situation (5–9). Even his closest friend has turned against him. The psalm ends with a prayer for healing and an expression of confidence (10–12).

The final verse is not really part of the psalm but is a doxology (or word of praise) which marks the end of Book I of the Psalms (see page 11 in Part One).

- Pray for those who have given much of their lives in the service of the poor and vulnerable and are now coming to the end of their lives. Pray especially for those who feel neglected by their friends and those who wonder if their life's work has been wasted.

> The two poles of human existence never alter:
> 'There is a time to weep and a time to laugh.'
> So the cry to God in the Psalms
> consists essentially of lament and praise.
>
> Claus Westermann

Book Two
Psalms 42 – 72

Psalms 42 and 43
The prayer of a disappointed pilgrim

*Why are you so full of heaviness, O my soul,
and why are you so disquieted within me?
Put your trust in God.*

Though this is usually printed and numbered as two psalms, it is in fact a single psalm with three stanzas, each ending with a refrain. The speaker is longing to go to Jerusalem, and find in worship there that closeness to God which refreshes his heart and soul (42:1–4). But he is ill, and so he cannot make his usual pilgrimage to Jerusalem. He has to stay at home, in the far north of Palestine, near Mount Hermon and the source of the River Jordan (42:6 in the Bible; 42:8 in *Common Worship*). He has happy memories of previous pilgrimages (42:4), but he is feeling very sad and despondent, and he urges himself to trust in God (the refrain: 42:5, 11; 43:5 in the Bible; 42:6–7, 13–14; 43:5–6 in *Common Worship*). He prays that by healing him God will vindicate him against his enemies and enable him to go to the 'holy hill' of Jerusalem once more (43:1–4).

The hymn 'As pants the hart for cooling streams' by Nahum Tate and Nicholas Brady is a metrical version of this psalm.

- Pray for those who because of illness or infirmity are unable to share in worship in church services, and miss it desperately.

Psalm 44
The cry of a nation
that has suffered a disastrous defeat in war

You have rejected us, and brought us to shame, and go not with our armies.

This prayer poem is built around a contrast between God's mighty acts for His people in the past (verses 1–8) and the terrible present when He no longer helps them (10–15 *Common Worship*;

10–16 Bible). The remembering of God's action for Israel in the past adds force to the protest that follows. Now God has allowed Israel to be defeated and humiliated. (The reference to 'scattered among the nations' suggests this may have been written at the exile and refers to the defeat by the Babylonian army in 587 BCE.) The repeated 'You ... you ... you' insists to God that He is responsible. Verses 18–22 emphasise the present disaster is not the result of Israel's betrayal or unfaithfulness. The psalm ends by calling on God to take action urgently.

- Pray for those who have seen their country defeated, the territory overrun by enemy soldiers, their homes and towns destroyed – in Bosnia, in Kosovo, in the Sudan, in Chechnya, Afghanistan and elsewhere.

Psalm 45
An anthem for a royal wedding

The sceptre of your kingdom is the sceptre of righteousness.

The first part of this psalm anthem (verses 2–9) is addressed to the King, in rather fulsome language. Then the anthem is addressed to the bride (10–12).

It ends with a blessing (16–17), promising children and a reputation in history. From a spiritual point of view the most significant aspect is the emphasis the psalm places on righteousness (or justice) as an essential quality of the King (4, 6–7).

• Pray for those who exercise authority and power in your country, that they may govern justly, protecting the weak and vulnerable, taking action for the good of the whole country rather than any sectional or personal interest.

Psalm 46
A song of Zion and a communal song of trust

God is our refuge and strength,
a very present help in trouble.

This psalm is both a song of Zion and the song of a community expressing its trust and confidence in God. It is in three stanzas. The first starts by setting out the theme of the whole psalm, the grounds for trust and confidence (verse 1). It affirms that trust in the face of potential catastrophes, a huge earthquake or a massive landslide (2–3).

The second stanza expresses that trust in the face of an attack by enemy nations on Jerusalem, the national capital and the city of God (4–6). Verse 7 is the refrain. The first phrase, 'the Lord of Hosts', speaks of the transcendent God, God in majesty. Jacob, son of Isaac, grandson of Abraham, was given the name Israel. The story is in Genesis 35:10–12. The people of Israel look to him as their ancestor and took their name from him. The second phrase in the refrain speaks of God in the nation's history.

The third stanza declares that after the attack has been repulsed the Lord destroys the weapons of war and brings in an era of peace throughout the world (8–10). The psalm ends with the refrain.

• Consider the worst disasters that could befall your family and your community – a natural disaster like an earthquake, the destruction of the place where you live by a nuclear strike. Hold these in your mind and affirm your trust in God by saying the verse quoted above.

Psalm 47
A song of the coming Kingdom of God

Sing praises to God, sing praises;
sing praises to our king, sing praises;
for God is the King of all the earth.

A hymn celebrating the reign of God as the King of all nations. It opens with a summons inviting all nations to praise God (verse 1). The grounds for this praise is set out, the victory He has won which establishes His universal reign (2–3). Verse 5 suggests the psalm was sung to accompany a religious ceremony in which the Lord's kingship was dramatised. (Compare psalm 24:7–10.) The call to praise is repeated (47:6) and the grounds for praise are rehearsed again (47:7–end).

• Think of situations which have been transformed, where injustice has been replaced by justice, bitterness and suspicion by mutual trust and respect. Can you think of any in your own experience? Some have happened on the world stage, such as the ending of apartheid in South Africa. Thank God for these glimpses of His rule as King.

Psalm 48
A song of Zion, delighting in the security God gives to His city

Great is the Lord and highly to be praised;
in the city of our God.

The psalm starts by praising the Lord as the God of Jerusalem (verses 1–3 in the Bible; 1–4 in *Common Worship*). When the heathen nations united to attack His city, they were routed (4–8 in the Bible; 5–8 in *Common Worship*). The city is called to rejoice in God's justice (verse 9). People are invited to go round the city and admire its buildings and to remember that God is its guardian and guide (12–end).

- Think of a church or a holy place that means a great deal to you. Picture it in your mind. Imagine you are walking around it and the different parts of it you see. Thank God for what He has given you through that building or that place.

Psalm 49
A Wisdom Psalm:
a meditation on the transience of life and wealth

Be not afraid if some grow rich
and the glory of their house increases,
for they will carry nothing away when they die,
nor will their glory follow after them.

Everyone is called to listen and ponder (verses 1–4). The theme of the psalm is introduced in verses 5–6: Why be afraid of wealthy, powerful people? No one is able to live forever or to take their wealth with them (7–15). The psalmist expresses confidence in God's deliverance (15 in the Bible; 16 in *Common Worship*), and encourages people not to envy the wealthy (16–end in the Bible; 17–end in *Common Worship*).

- Are there times when you are resentful of the success and happiness of others? If so, acknowledge it to yourself and to God. Ask Him for a spirit of gratitude for His goodness to you that will sweep away your resentment.

Psalm 50
A solemn warning against taking God lightly

Gather to me my faithful,
who have sealed my covenant with sacrifice.

The language of this psalm suggests that it comes from an order of service or liturgy. The references to 'covenant' in verses 5 and 16 suggest it may have been a service remembering and renewing the covenant the Lord made with His people at Sinai (see 'Covenant' in the Glossary, page 46). It is a solemn warning against taking lightly the covenant relationship with God.

The opening verses picture God convening an assembly or court of law (verses 1-4). Then God speaks (5–6). First He addresses those who are religious in a conventional way. They take part in religious services but have little sense of who God really is. To them He asserts his sovereign independence. He does not need their offerings and sacrifices. On the contrary, they need to acknowledge their dependence on Him.

Then He turns to 'the wicked', that is, those who pay lip service to God, but whose lying, deceit and sexual unfaithfulness break the covenant they profess (16–22). For them He has a solemn warning, but His final message is one that promises blessing.

- Reflect on the 'otherness' of God. How often do you – how often does the Church – take God lightly, assume He will be generous to us in a fairly undemanding way, treat Him as if He were just like us?

Psalm 51
A cry for forgiveness that comes from the heart

Make me a clean heart, O God,
and renew a right spirit within me.

One of the Seven Psalms (see page 21), psalm 51 is the deepest and most heartfelt prayer for forgiveness in the psalms, and perhaps in the whole Bible. The psalmist feels intensely keenly how wrong his behaviour has been.

Psalm 51 is said at the main service on Ash Wednesday in *Common Worship*. In the *Book of Common Prayer* three separate verses are included in the opening sentences at Morning and Evening Prayer that lead into confession. It is a psalm that we can use to draw us into penitence.

The psalm starts at once with a plea for forgiveness, calling on God to show His abundant mercy (verses 1–2). The psalmist moves quickly into confessing his sin (3–5). He uses intense language so as to move God to forgive him. He is conscious of the difference between what is external and superficial and what is inward and deep (6 in the Bible; 7 in *Common Worship*), and he is seeking for a profound experience of forgiveness.

The plea of verses 1–2 is repeated and developed (7–12 in the Bible; 8–13 in *Common Worship*). It is now a positive request, that the whole person may be changed. He is not simply asking for sin to be removed, but for a new spirit and a new life of joy. The language reflects the message of the prophets of the exile (e.g. Ezekiel 36:25–27).

He goes on to make the vow or promise of what he will do if his prayer is answered, a vow often found in laments (13–17 in the Bible; 14–18 in *Common Worship*). Part of this promise is to help others to find the way to repentance and forgiveness.

In early times the vow involved both praise and the offering of a sacrifice, but the critique of sacrifice by the prophets seen in, for example, Hosea 6:6 and Micah 6:6–8 made it less significant. With the destruction of the Temple, sacrifice ceased for a long time.

The last two verses are a postscript, a prayer for the rebuilding of Jerusalem, which will make possible the restoration of sacrifice.

Psalm 51 expresses the prophetic insight that a new beginning, a new relationship with God, can only come when guilt is forgiven. Forgiveness brings about the change to a new and joyful life in fellowship with God.

The title in the Hebrew Bible links this psalm with King David. He was rebuked by the prophet Nathan because he had committed adultery with Bathsheba and arranged for her husband to be killed in battle so that he could marry her. The account given in 2 Samuel 11 – 12 is well worth reading.

• Ponder for a few moments on those things in your life of which you are most ashamed, or about which you feel most guilty. Confess them to God, and then ask for forgiveness and His gift of new life, using verses 9–12.

Psalm 52
A cry of confidence that evil will be punished and good vindicated

You love evil rather than good;
falsehood rather than the word of truth.

The title links this psalm with an event in the life of David when he was escaping from King Saul who was trying to find him and kill him. Doeg told Saul that the priest Ahimelech had befriended David. Saul was furious at this and ordered that Ahimelech should be executed, but his servants were unwilling to strike a priest. Doeg then killed him. The account is in 1 Samuel 22:6–19.

The bitter angry tone of verses 1–4 may reflect anger at Doeg's readiness to kill the priest of the Lord. But the psalmist is confident that evil will receive just retribution from the Lord (5–7), and that those who trust in the Lord will flourish (8–9).

- Remember those who have seen honest people humiliated, injured or even killed by people who are dishonest, treacherous or violent. They may be struggling with the sense that the world is unjust, and they cannot trust in God's justice. Imagine their feelings and pray for them.

Psalm 53
A lament over the folly and wickedness of this age

*Everyone has turned back; all alike have
become corrupt;
there is none that does good, no, not one.*

This psalm is almost identical to psalm 14 except
that in this psalm Elohim (God) is addressed and in
psalm 14 it is Yahweh (the Lord) who is addressed.
It probably had been included in two different collections of psalms which were both incorporated in
the Book of Psalms.

The psalmist starts by grieving over the folly and
corruption of society. It is a deeply depressing
picture of a society rotten with corruption and
oppression (verses 1–4). There follows a confident
assertion that the Lord will take action to overthrow the oppressors (5). The psalm ends with a
prayer that yearns for the Lord to act.

• Think of those things that give you a sense of
  despair about society – for example, the widespread use of drugs and the activities of drugpushers, the extent of assaults, rapes and other
  violent crimes, the casual way some people abandon wives, husbands or partners of many years.
  Bring them into the presence of God.

Psalm 54
A cry for help in a time of great danger

Behold God is my helper.

This is another psalm linked by its title to the period in David's life when he was on the run from Saul. He was in hiding in the Wilderness of Ziph, a hilly, thickly wooded area to the west of the Dead Sea. The local people told Saul he was there. Saul was closing in on David. It was a very frightening time for him. (See 1 Samuel 23:14–29.)

The psalm opens with a heartfelt cry to God to listen and to help (verses 1–3). But then comes an expression of confidence that God will act (4–5), leading to a promise to give Him thanks (6–7).

• Think of people whom you find oppressive, who tend to crush you, even though they may not intend to and do not realise what they are doing. Pray that your relationship with them may be changed and that the Lord will give you the strength to do your part in making that change.

Psalm 55
A cry for protection from enemies

It was not an open enemy that reviled me,
for then I could have borne it.
But it was even you, one like myself,
my companion and my own familiar friend.

Among a number of psalms that are prayers for protection and deliverance from enemies, this one is marked out by its intense sense of betrayal. The enemy who is now threatening is not a stranger but an old friend, with whom the speaker enjoyed conversation and fellowship (e.g. verses 12–14, 20–21 in the Bible; 13–15, 22–23 in *Common Worship*). The result is anguish of heart and an intense fear of being killed (5).

• Pray for people who feel betrayed by someone with whom they had a close relationship. It may be the result of a marriage that has ended in bitterness and recrimination, or perhaps a friendship or business partnership. Pray for them as they struggle with pain and resentment.

Psalm 56
A prayer for protection when enemies are on every side

Have mercy on me, O God, for they trample over me.

This is another in the series of psalms linked with David's escape from King Saul who was looking for an opportunity to kill him. To escape Saul David left the country but was held as prisoner by the Philistines (see 1 Samuel 21:10 – 22:1).

The feeling of being surrounded by enemies is powerfully expressed in verses 1–7, but within this urgent cry for help there is an expression of confidence in the Lord (3–4). He appeals that his enemies may receive the retribution they deserve (7) and renews his expression of confidence (9–11). He ends the psalm by promising to make a thank-offering when God has answered his prayer.

• Pray for those who are constantly afraid of what powerful people may do to them, those who are being bullied at work or at school, those who are receiving hate mail or threatening telephone calls, those who face racial prejudice.

Psalm 57
A prayer for refuge in a time of danger

*In the shadow of your wings will I take refuge
until the storm of destruction has passed by.*

This psalm is linked to the previous one by its title.
David has escaped from the Philistines in Gath and
is now hiding from Saul in a cave in the hills, where
he is joined by a group of supporters (see 1 Samuel
22:1–2). The threat from Saul is still very real, but
at least he has his friends around him.

The mood of the psalm is more confident, the cry
for help less urgent. The enemies are still there, as
fierce and dangerous as lions with sharp teeth, but
there is a strong sense that refuge and safety is
found in God. The psalm is marked by two features
– the refrain of praise at the end of each section,
and the thanksgiving song in the second half of the
psalm, sung in anticipation of God's answer to
prayer. (This thanksgiving song is also the first part
of psalm 108.)

- Pray for those who for the time being have found
  refuge from a violent and dangerous situation:
  battered women and their children in a hostel,
  asylum seekers who have fled from their own
  countries.

Psalm 58
An angry protest against the injustice and cruelty of those in power

Do you indeed speak justly, you mighty?
Do you rule the peoples with equity?

This psalm is a bitter, passionate protest of those who are weak and vulnerable against the way powerful people exploit them, cheat them, oppress them (verses 1–5). It may remind us of harsh dictators or military regimes which exploit the people of their countries. The cry to God is to put things right, to break their power (6) and give them their just deserts. Only then will people be able to say, 'Truly there is a God who judges in the earth' (11).

Some of the language used in this psalm is horrendous. We need to remember it is 'a cry for rescue uttered by the victims of criminal brutality' (Erich Zenger). It comes from people who are terrified to death. They are not calling for revenge so much as for the restoration of justice. Those who are guilty of war crimes need to be tried and condemned.

- Pray for people today who are weak and vulnerable and are treated cruelly or exploited by dictators, military regimes, rich élites or large commercial companies. (If possible, remember an actual situation you have heard about, and pray for those involved.)

Psalm 59
A prayer to be rescued from the threat of violence

Rescue me from my enemies, O my God.

This is the fifth in a series of psalms linked with David's flight from King Saul. The others are psalms 52, 54, 56 and 57. This comes from an earlier stage than the previous ones. David's house is being watched by members of Saul's entourage who have orders to kill him (see 1 Samuel 19: 11–18).

A sense of threat and menace pervades this psalm. The armed men lying in wait are pictured as a pack of scavenging dogs who prowl around, growling and searching for meat to eat.

The first part of the psalm alternates between cries for help, 'Rescue me ... Save me ... come to my aid', and descriptions of the situation (verses 3–4, 6–7 in the Bible; 7–8 in *Common Worship*). There follows a song of trust and confidence (8–10 in the Bible; 9–11 in *Common Worship*).

Then comes an appeal that these enemies may receive their just deserts. The appeal is not for the personal gain of the psalmist, but that God will show publicly that He rules by arresting and convicting those who are doing evil.

Then the sense of threat intrudes again, and the danger is re-emphasised before the final verse brings the speaker's promise to give thanks and praise to God.

- Think today of the enemies not as external but as internal, the fears, the resentments, the lusts, the despair, that can so easily consume our thoughts. Pray for yourself. Pray for those who often feel overwhelmed by 'the dogs' within.

Psalm 60
A national lament after defeat in battle

O God, you have cast us off and broken us.

The title links this psalm with David, but it is difficult to connect with any event described in the Books of Samuel.

The first part of this psalm is the pained cry of a people who have been defeated and humiliated, perhaps by the Edomites (verse 9). The language, with its repeated 'you ... you ... you ...', makes it clear that God is held responsible for this defeat. It is the result of His action.

This is followed by an oracle (6–8), a statement made in God's name, perhaps by a Temple official. God declares that He rules over both the land of Israel (the places named in 6–7) and also over Israel's traditional enemies (named in 8). The former are given symbols of honour – helmet and sceptre – the latter menial ones – wash-pot and sandal, but in both cases it is God who gives them.

The psalm ends with a prayer for help (9–11) and an affirmation of confidence in victory through God's power (12).

• Think of those countries where relationships between them and your own country are uneasy, difficult, perhaps hostile. Pray for those countries and their leaders, and for these relationships.

Psalm 61
The prayer of an exile

From the end of the earth I call to you.

The plaintive tone of the opening verses expresses something of the pain of an exile. Verse 2 quoted above implies that this is the prayer of someone who is far from the land of Israel. Perhaps the person praying is a prisoner of war seized in a raid by an invading army and carried away, like the Israelite slave-girl who was a servant of the Syrian army commander Naaman. (The story is in 2 Kings 5.) But even when she is far from her homeland her thoughts are of her people and her king (verses 6–7).

Her prayer for the king shows that the psalm cannot come from the time of the main exile in Babylon when there was no king in Israel, but from the time of the kingdom (see Part One, pp. 6–7).

The psalm brings together prayer for oneself (1–4) and prayer for the community or nation, represented by the king (6–7). In doing this it offers a good guideline for personal daily prayer.

- Pray for yourself, for what you most need. Pray for your country, that its national life may be marked by steadfast love – reliability in caring for each other.

Psalm 62
A song of trust and confidence in God's protection

On God alone my soul in stillness waits.

There are times when waiting is an essential element in trusting – being prepared to wait to allow God to take action rather than feeling one must do something oneself.

The psalm starts with an expression of confidence in God (verses 1–2). Then the speaker's threatening, potentially very frightening situation, is described (3–4), but the expression of confidence is repeated (5–6). The speaker then calls on people everywhere to put their trust in God, and not to rely on their power or wealth or on dishonest practices (8–12).

- Say verse 1 as a prayer, and then think about those things that you find most disturbing and most frightening, repeating verse 1 as an expression of your trust in God.

Psalm 63
A song of yearning for the presence of God

O God, you are my God, I seek you,
my soul thirsts for you; my flesh faints for you,
as in a dry and weary land where there is no
water.

The distinctive feature of this delightful psalm is its strong sense of longing and yearning for God's presence. The psalmist longs for this, as the parched traveller longs for water in the desert (verse 1). When this longing for God is met it is as satisfying as a rich feast (6 *Common Worship*; 5 Bible). The intensely personal spirituality leads to a trust which recognises threats and danger, but is completely confident in God's protection (10–11 *Common Worship*; 9–10 Bible).

The last verse may be an addition designed to adapt this very personal expression of spirituality to make it suitable for public worship.

• Read verses 1–7 again slowly, savouring them in your mind and heart. Repeat any verse or phrase that strikes you as a prayer to God.

Psalm 64
A prayer for protection from verbal attacks

Hear my voice, O God, in my complaint.

The shape of this psalm is very typical of laments; a cry for help (verses 1–2), a description of the speaker's painful experience (3–6), leading into an expression of confidence that God will answer this prayer (7–9). Its distinctive feature is the nature of the threat – the words the enemies use (3–4) – malicious gossip, false accusation, verbal abuse, character assassination.

• Pray for those whose words are influential, who write what many read and speak where many hear. Pray for them when they are tempted to use their influence to run down other people. Pray for those who are the victims of unfair criticism or malicious accusation.

Psalm 65
A community's thanksgiving for a good harvest

*May the meadows be clothed with flocks of
sheep
and the valleys stand so thick with corn
that they shall laugh and sing.*

The psalm starts with people gathering in the
Temple for an act of praise in which they acknowledge their guilt and celebrate forgiveness (verses
1–4). They sing their praises to God as the One
who created the world (5–7) and makes the earth
fertile with plentiful crops and livestock (8–13).

Verse 5 (4 in *Common Worship*) has the lovely
phrase describing God as 'the hope of all the ends
of the earth', a vivid expression of the world-wide
scope of God's salvation. This cosmic perspective is
the key theme in the central part of the psalm.

• Thank God for his blessings on your country, for
  its landscape, its hills and valleys, fields and
  rivers, and for the fertility of its soil.

Psalm 66
A song of thanksgiving, communal and personal

We went through fire and water,
but you brought us out into a place of liberty.

This psalm links together two songs of thanksgiving. Firstly there is a song of the community which has been through a painful experience of oppression and suffering. Then there is a personal song of thanksgiving.

The psalm starts by calling on the whole earth to worship God, singing his praises and declaring what He has done. The statement about turning the sea into dry land (verse 6 in the Bible; 5 in *Common Worship*) would seem to be a reference to the Exodus (see Glossary, page 43). The story of what the people of Israel went through, the terrible situation from which God rescued them, is told (10–12 in the Bible; 9–11 in *Common Worship*). (This telling of the story is a characteristic feature of songs of thanksgiving.)

The second part of the psalm is a personal song of thanksgiving. The speaker calls on people to listen to this story of God's answer to prayer.

• Think of countries and peoples who have suffered greatly and come through it, for example those who lived under Communist rulers or under dictators now deposed. Give thanks for them and with them.

Psalm 67
Thanksgiving for a good harvest

The earth has yielded its increase;
God, our God, has blessed us.

(NRSV)

In just seven verses this psalm manages to include praise (verses 3, 5), appreciation of God's generosity (6), and prayer for his continuing blessing (1–2, 7). World-wide in its vision ('all nations ... all peoples'), it recognises that justice is an essential aspect of God's action (4).

This psalm was the inspiration of H. F. Lyte's hymn 'God of mercy, God of grace'.

- Imagine yourself walking around a supermarket and picture the rich variety of delicious foods that you can choose from to enjoy for your meals over the coming week. Thank God for His generous and abundant provision, and pray for a fairer sharing of the earth's resources.

Psalm 68
A song of praise to God who cares for His people

Father of the fatherless, defender of widows.

As this is a fairly long psalm, you may prefer to read it in
two parts, verses 1–20 and 21–35.

It is difficult to find an overall shape to this psalm,
which seems rather disjointed with several separate
sections. One broad theme runs through it. God
cares for His people, especially the most vulnerable
– orphans, widows, the homeless and prisoners
(verses 5–6). He looked after them when they jour-
neyed through the wilderness of Sinai (7–14 in the
Bible; 7–13 in *Common Worship*), providing for
them (8–10), giving them victory over their enemies
(11–12). He has chosen Mount Zion for His
dwelling place (15–18 in the Bible; 14–17 in
Common Worship). Processions enter His sanctuary (24–27 in the Bible; 23–26 in *Common
Worship*). It is right to sing His praises (4, 32).

• Pray for all people described in verses 5–6:
  children without parents, widows, the homeless,
  prisoners, and for organisations that work for
  them.

Psalm 69
The cry of someone who is overwhelmed
and about to go under

Save me, O God,
for the waters have come up to my neck.

As this is a fairly long psalm, you may prefer to read it in
two parts, verses 1–15 and 16–36 in the Bible, 1–16 and
17–38 in *Common Worship*.

The psalm starts with a cry for help. The vivid language with its picture of someone drowning gives a sense of great urgency to the prayers. To sink in mud or quicksand and to feel the waters rising up is a terrifying experience.

He, or perhaps she, is being falsely accused by a large number of people who hate him, though he acknowledges he is not without fault (verse 6 *Common Worship*; 5 Bible). In his prayer to the Lord he presses the point that it is 'for your sake' he is facing this hostility. The implication is it is the Lord's responsibility to take action to save his loyal servant.

He then launches into his complaint with a description of the hatred he is facing. Verse 9 (10 in *Common Worship*) suggests he may have been very active in working for the Temple. (It is quoted in John 2:17, referring to Jesus.) The description is interrupted by a prayer which is marked by urgent, insistent pleading. He then returns to his complaint.

Verse 21 (verse 23 in *Common Worship*), with its reference to drinking vinegar, is seen by all four Gospel writers as referring to Jesus being given vinegar to drink on the cross. So this psalm is set to be said or sung on Good Friday.

The psalmist then begins to curse his enemies. The curses in the psalms are very difficult to understand, but the comments in the section 'Cries for justice' on pages 38–45 in Part One may be helpful.

After a final cry to God, asking for protection, the psalm, like many laments, ends with a song of praise and thanksgiving. The anger and hate expressed in the curses are not the last word. The psalmist is able to move beyond them. The final verses, with their reference to the rebuilding of Judah, make this personal lament suitable for the corporate worship of a weak and oppressed people.

• In a short time of silence remember Jesus on the cross, surrounded by people full of hatred towards Him, shouting abuse at him, accusing Him. Thank Him that by accepting this anger and hatred He overcame it and opened for us the way to a new dimension of life. Pray for those who are having to face hatred and false accusation now.

Psalm 70
An urgent cry for help

O Lord, make haste to help me.

The key feature of this short psalm is its sense of urgency. It starts by asking the Lord to 'make haste' (verse 1) and ends by pleading with Him 'not to delay'. It does not have time to describe the trouble the speaker is in beyond a brief reference to threatening enemies.

This psalm offers phrases we can use as 'arrow' prayers at times when we need to take immediate action and give all our attention to what we have to do.

This psalm is almost identical to the closing verses of psalm 40.

• Think of three or four people who need urgent help, three or four situations where change is needed quickly to save people from suffering. Pray short arrow prayers for each of these.

Psalm 71
An old person's prayer for protection

Do not cast me away in the time of old age.

Two verses – 9 and 18 – show us the age of the speaker. It is an elderly person whose powers are failing, and whose enemies are delighted about this (verses 9–11).

The psalm starts with a cry for help (1–3). Then the speaker finds confidence in remembering that she (or he) has trusted in God from her earliest days and He has always proved reliable (4–6). But her failing powers and the malice of her enemies leads her to cry again for help (12–13).

Then, confident that God will answer her prayer, she begins to praise Him (14–21). At the end of the psalm her praise bursts out in song (22–24).

• Pray for elderly people who are finding it difficult to come to terms with their inability to do the things they used to do, and are perhaps frightened at their increasing dependence on others.

Psalm 72
A royal psalm:
a prayer for God's blessing on the King

May he defend the poor among the people,
deliver the children of the needy and crush the
oppressor.

This prayer for God's blessing on the King goes at
once to the heart of the matter. The most important
quality for a King is justice and righteousness (verse
1). And the people who most need justice are the
poor (2). They are weak and vulnerable, and those
who are more powerful are always likely to take
advantage of them. Note how often words like
'poor', 'needy', and 'weak' occur in this psalm. The
result of this justice will be prosperity (3).

So the psalm weaves together three themes:

- Justice and the protection of the poor and vulnerable (verses 1–4, 12–14).
- Prosperity, reflected in good harvests (3, 16).
- Power, a large empire and victory over enemies
  (8–11).

These themes are linked. An essential element in
'judging', justice and righteousness was that the
ruler protected the poor and vulnerable from

powerful people who tried to exploit and oppress them. Such righteousness would be rewarded by God, who would give good harvests and prosperity, and make the whole nation powerful.

The King was a 'corporate personality', the representative of his people. A good King meant a good people. If the King was evil, then the whole people became corrupt.

The prayers of this psalm give a vision of kingship which contribute to our Christian understanding of the Kingdom of God of which Jesus spoke in the Gospels.

The last verses are a doxology which marks the end of Book II of the Psalms.

• Pray for the Queen (or your Head of State) and all those who act in her name, members of the Government, judges, etc. Pray that they may take effective action to ensure that the poor and vulnerable get a fair deal, and are not ignored and neglected because they have little power in society.

Book Three
Psalms 73 – 89

Psalm 73
The story of a change of heart and mind

*I was envious of the proud ...
my heart became embittered.*

Psalm 73 is a most distinctive and remarkable
psalm. In a thoughtful and reflective way it tells the
story of how the speaker became jealous and bitter
at the success of others, and how a new vision
enabled him to break out of his resentment and find
a renewed trust in God.

It starts with a statement of faith (verse 1). God
is good to those who are pure in heart. Verses 2–16
then state the problem: actual experience does not
match up to this belief. The speaker sees selfish,
greedy and arrogant people being very successful,

and he is burning with envy. The language gives a vivid picture of the way he is almost obsessed. It is full of 'them' – how awful they are and how prosperous they are. He expresses his deep doubt with some bitterness (13–14) but also his sense of loyalty to God (15).

The turning point comes in verse 17. He goes to worship God, and he begins to see things differently. He gains a new awareness of the consequence of an evil life (18–20), and realises how stupid he has been (21–22). He feels a new appreciation of God's goodness to him (23–26).

In the first part of the psalm God is spoken about – in the third person (1, 11). But after his change of heart the speaker addresses God directly – 'you'. Reflection is turned into prayer.

At the end he sets out his conclusions (27–28).

• Pray for those who feel very keenly the unfairness of the success of those who are selfish, greedy and arrogant – include yourself if that is how you feel. Pray they may have the insight to see God is far more valuable than any worldly success.

Psalm 74
A nation's cry of mourning
over the destruction of its Temple

They set fire to your holy place.

This psalm is a nation's lament over the destruction of the Temple by the Babylonian army when it captured Jerusalem in 586 BCE. The Temple, the centre of the nation's spiritual life, the lynchpin of Israel's religion, is totally ruined. The supreme symbol of God's presence has gone.

The psalm starts not with the Temple but with God, begging Him to explain why He has abandoned His people (verse 1), pleading with Him to remember the past (2), and to look at their present situation (3).

Then follows a vivid description of the enemy soldiers smashing the Temple and setting it on fire. This is a way of pressing the Lord to take action. It is not only the Temple but all the places of worship throughout the country that have been destroyed by fire. The speaker emphasises that they are not just 'our' enemies, but 'yours'. God is allowing Himself to be dishonoured by what has happened.

Then, in verse 12 (verse 11 in *Common Worship*), the tone changes. God's great actions in the past are recited both in the exodus from Egypt and in creation. Note how often the word 'you' is used.

On the basis of this, the appeal to God is renewed with a series of imperatives – 'Remember ... Look ... Arise ...' God is called on to take action.

There is no final song or vow of thanksgiving. Perhaps that would imply more hope than people are able to feel in their present miserable plight. The psalm ends by calling on God not to forget.

- All over the world there are people who have seen their homes and towns destroyed and their friends and families murdered, often in forms of communal violence or so-called 'ethnic cleansing' – in East Timor, the Sudan, Kosovo, Bosnia, Sri Lanka, Rwanda and Afghanistan. Pray for them in their grief and shock.

Psalm 75
A communal thanksgiving

God alone is judge,
he puts down one and raises up another.

The psalm starts by giving thanks to God for His wonderful deeds (verse 1). Then an oracle is pronounced in God's name warning the arrogant not to boast and toss their horns (like an ill-tempered bull) (2-5). People respond by expressing their faith that God alone is judge and that He will enforce justice (6–8). Those who have wronged others will get 'a cup of their own medicine'.

The psalm ends with prayer and with a pledge, but it is not clear who is the speaker: Is it the worshipper? Or is it perhaps the King?

- Pray for the government of your country, that they may take effective action to prevent greedy or angry people from harming others, and to make restitution to those who have been wronged.

Psalm 76
A song of Zion celebrating God's victory

God rose up to establish judgement,
to save all the oppressed of the earth.

(NRSV)

The psalm starts by announcing God's victory (verses 1–3). ('Salem' is a short form of 'Jerusalem'.) It moves into a hymn of praise, addressed to God, describing the victory (4–6). This seems to be celebrating victory in a specific battle when an army threatening Jerusalem was defeated, but we do not know which battle it refers to.

Then from verse 7 the focus shifts from the specific to the universal. God is going to 'save all the oppressed and meek of the earth' (9). The psalm ends by calling on people to accept the rule of this awesome God, making vows and bringing Him gifts (10–12).

• Pray for the meek and the oppressed, for those unable or unwilling to fight to gain fair treatment from those who are ruthless in taking advantage of them.

Psalm 77
The cry of someone who is grieving over his nation's plight

Will the Lord cast us off forever?

The psalm starts with a cry of grief that can find no comfort (verses 1–4). The speaker lies awake at night, sleepless and in despair. He then moves into a meditation or reflection, questioning whether God has lost interest and ceased to love His people

(5–10). The contrast between the past and the present is almost intolerable. He puts his bewilderment and his doubts into words (7–10).

But his thoughts move on. He calls to mind what God has done for His people in the past. He no longer speaks about God ('he', 'his') and begins to speak to God ('you', 'your') – see verse 11. His mood changes. Meditation turns into praise (13 onwards). The psalm turns into a hymn of thanksgiving and praise, telling the story of God's amazing intervention, using vivid poetic images. God's power is seen in the way His thunder makes the earth shake. The reference to Moses and his brother Aaron makes it clear that what he is talking about is the Exodus.

By the end of the psalm the 'I' that was so dominant in the first half has disappeared and the psalm is full of 'you'.

• What is it in the life of your country that you grieve over? The treatment of those who are mentally ill? Of refugees? Of unborn children? Express your grief in a specific prayer to the Lord.

Psalm 78
A historical recital contrasting God's blessing and Israel's faithlessness

Verses 1–31

They forgot what He had done.

The psalm starts in the style of a teacher of wisdom, calling people to listen to his teaching (verses 1–10). The Lord has commanded His people to teach their children through the generations (5–8).

The psalm then begins to tell the story of the events of the Exodus (12–16) and of the years of travelling in the wilderness that followed. It is a recitation of God's dealings with Israel. He is the prime actor in the story, whether in blessing or in judgement. There is a sharp contrast between the wonderful things that God has done (12–16) and Israel's rebelliousness and lack of faith (17–22). Israel is stubborn (8), forgetful of what God has done for them (11).

The history of Israel's journey through the wilderness continues (23 onwards).

- Reflect for a few moments on your own discipleship and on the life of the people of God, the

Church of Christ. Where do you consider the people of God are faithless today? Confess this to God, asking Him for forgiveness and for strength to put things right.

Verses 32–55

How often they rebelled against Him.

The second part of the psalm, like the first, sees the whole of Israel's history as under the controlling providence of God. The relationship between God and Israel is the key to interpreting historical events. Israel's refusal to serve Him, His judgement and His mercy explain the nation's experience over the centuries.

Israel's faithlessness is seen as a continuing saga. Like rebellious children, they grieved God's heart (verse 40). Verses 44–51 describe the disasters that struck the land of Egypt in the months before the Exodus. They are often called 'the plagues of Egypt', and are seen as God's judgement on Egypt for holding the people of Israel in slavery and not releasing them. It was God who brought Israel out of Egypt (52–53) and led them into their land (54–55).

• Think again of the people of God, the Church of Christ. Pray that the people of God may keep in their memory the great things God has done and rejoice in serving Him faithfully.

Verses 56–72

> *He chose David also, His servant ...*
> *that he might shepherd Jacob His people*
> *and Israel His inheritance.*

In spite of God's generous gift of the Promised Land to the people of Israel, they still turned away from Him and worshipped idols (verses 56–58). In judgement He allowed other nations to attack Israel with sword and fire (59–64), but then He stepped in to drive the enemies out (65–66).

The final section of the psalm emphasises that it was by God's free choice that David the shepherd became King of Israel. (See 'Ephraim', 'Judah' and 'David' in the Glossary, pages 47–50.) David came from the tribe of Judah. Ephraim was one of the sons of Joseph. The tribe of Ephraim's lands are in the north, so that they became part of the northern kingdom that was destroyed by the Assyrian army in 721 BCE.

There is a similar emphasis on God's free choice in the words of Jesus to His disciples at the Last Supper: 'You did not choose me, but I chose you' (John 15:16).

- Reflect on the responsibilities that God entrusts to those whom He chooses, and the responsibilities He has given to you and to your church. Pray that you may be able to carry out the mission and vocation to which God has called you.

Psalm 79
The cry of a nation defeated in war and left in ruins

O God, the heathen have come into your heritage;
your holy temple have they defiled
and made Jerusalem a heap of stones.

This psalm emerges out of one of the most terrible of human experiences, defeat in war. Many people have been killed and left unburied (verse 33), the most sacred place has been desecrated, homes have been reduced to ruins (1). It is highly likely it refers to the destruction of Jerusalem and the Temple by the Babylonian army in 586 BCE.

The language is urgent and passionate, reflecting the horror of the situation. God's involvement in the disaster is emphasised from the first verse. It is His heritage the heathen have entered, His Temple they have defiled.

But the disaster is recognised as God's judgement. The psalm prays for forgiveness, for the wiping away of sins (8–9).

Together with the cry for help goes the cry for retribution (see the section 'Cries for justice: cries for retribution' in Part One, pages 38–45). It expresses the rage, the longing to hurt and destroy felt by those who have seen their families killed and their homes destroyed. But this longing is submitted to the Lord. Both the prayer for forgiveness and the cry for vengeance are addressed to Him. The psalm both sees the tenderness of God, listening to the sighing of the prisoners, and also calls on Him to be ruthless.

But the psalm ends on a note of hope. The final verse anticipates that the Lord will put things right, and that His people will have cause to thank and praise Him.

- Pray for those who have seen their families and friends killed, their homes destroyed, their sacred places desecrated. Pray for them in their grief, their pain and anguish, and in the anger and hatred they feel.

Psalm 80
A national lament and a prayer for restoration

You brought a vine out of Egypt ...
and when it had taken root, it filled the land.

The psalm starts by calling on God as the 'Shepherd of Israel', a lovely phrase that echoes psalm 23, 'The Lord is my shepherd'. It is a call for help that is repeated several times during the psalm. Ephraim, Benjamin and Manasseh are in the north, suggesting that this psalm is a response to the invasion of the northern kingdom (see 'Kingdom' in the Glossary, p. 51) by the Assyrian army in the eighth century BCE.

The humiliation that the nation is experiencing is seen as God turning away from them and ignoring them. The psalm speaks to Him directly, 'you ... you ... you', holding Him responsible.

The comparison of the people of God to a vine is used by a number of writers in the Old Testament. As well as this psalm it appears in Isaiah 5:1–7 and Ezekiel 19:10–14. Jesus also uses it in the parable of the vineyard in Mark 12:1–11 and uses the vine as a picture of His relationship with His disciples at the Last Supper in John 15:1–11.

It is used here to press home the contrast between

the way God has cared for His people in the past and the present disastrous situation. 'Why destroy what you have built?' is the argument used to re-inforce the appeal.

The psalm ends with a prayer, calling on God to turn, to cherish the vine He has planted and restore His people.

- Pray for the Church of God in places where it has suffered greatly, with churches being destroyed and church people being arrested and imprisoned. These include, among others, the Sudan, East Timor, and some of the former Soviet Republics in central Asia.

Psalm 81
'The word of the Lord', calling Israel to listen

O Israel, if you would but listen to me.

This psalm comes from the order of service (or liturgy) for a festival (see verse 3). It was probably the Feast of the Booths or Tabernacles when people lived for a week in booths or tabernacles made out of branches of trees to commemorate the journey of the people of Israel through the wilderness.

It starts with a song, calling on people to sing to

God with joy in their hearts (1–3). Verses 4–5 introduce the theme of the Law or Torah (see Part One, page 28). Then in verse 6 another voice speaks. Think of someone in a church service reading from one of the Old Testament prophets declaring the word of the Lord.

People are reminded of what the Lord has done for them in the past (6–7) and of His demand for their loyalty (8–10). But they have not listened (11–12). If they are willing to listen, then the Lord is ready to bless them and they will enjoy freedom and prosperity (13–16).

- Think of your country or nation. Which are the areas of national and social life which are clearly not following the Lord's ways? Pray for these areas of life and for those who are working to reform and renew them.

Psalm 82
A pronouncement of judgement

Rescue the weak and the poor;
deliver them from the hand of the wicked.

This psalm pictures God taking his seat in court and pronouncing judgement (verse 1). Those who exercise authority and power are condemned for failing to defend the right of the weak and the poor, and not protecting them from those who exploit them (2–3).

Just who is coming under God's judgement is not clear. They are addressed as 'gods' and 'children of the Most High' (6). Are they human rulers, given this title as God's deputies? Or are they heathen 'gods'? Whichever they are, the values this psalm expresses are clear. A central task of those in power is to maintain justice by protecting the weak from powerful and unscrupulous people who will take advantage of them.

The final verse calls on God to take action and to come in judgement.

• Pray for wise judgement on the part of the government of your country and of other nations with which it has close relations. Pray that they may use their power as the government to protect and provide for the poor and the vulnerable.

Psalm 83
A scream of protest from a people whose very existence is threatened

They say 'Come, let us destroy them as a nation, that the name of Israel be remembered no more.'

An alliance of nations has been formed, encircling Israel, with the intention of attacking and destroying it (verses 2–8). Israel's existence as a nation is threatened. It is surrounded by enemies. In the face of this terrifying threat, this psalm is a scream of protest. The violence of the language reflects the intense fear that this threat causes (9–10).

The first part (1–8) argues that Israel's fate and the Lord's are inseparable. If Israel is threatened, the Lord is threatened. If the nations are conspiring against Israel, they are conspiring against the Lord (2–5).

The second part (9–18) calls directly on the Lord to act. But the call is not primarily for the nations' destruction but their transformation. The prayer is that they may experience the power of God and His judgement on them, so that they come to seek Him (16) and come to know that He is the Lord (18).

• Think of a situation in which people who are

weak are being victimised and oppressed by those who are powerful, and cry out in protest to God that he will restrain the oppressors and strip them of their power.

Psalm 84
A song of Zion, the joy of pilgrims

My heart and my flesh rejoice in the living God.

The distinctive feature of this psalm is the intense love it expresses for the Temple as the place of meeting with the living God. The first part of the psalm is full of deep longing to be in the Temple. It sounds as though the speaker lives far away like the writer of psalm 42/43.

The second part is about the journey. The speaker imagines pilgrims on their way to Jerusalem, travelling along 'the highways to Zion', and through the valley with its springs. The thought of Zion leads her into a prayer for the anointed King who lives in Jerusalem. Because he has responsibility for protecting the poor, he is the guardian of pilgrims as they are vulnerable on their journey.

In the third part she thinks of them on their arrival at Jerusalem, going into the courts of the Temple. She recalls the blessings the Lord God gives to all those who trust in Him and live with integrity.

- Pray for yourself, for Christian friends and neighbours and for the whole people of God, that we may have a deep longing for a closer relationship with God and find joy and delight in drawing near to Him.

Psalm 85
A nation's prayer for restoration

Mercy and truth will meet together,
righteousness and peace will kiss each other.

(Author's translation)

The psalm starts by recalling the Lord's goodness to His people in times past (verses 1–3), but this is a way of leading into the main point, an argument encouraging Him to act now. Then, in verses 4–7, comes the request, the prayer. The nation has suffered some disaster or setback. It is not described, so we do not know what has happened, but it is seen as a mark of God's displeasure. The prayer is for restoration, for revival, for God's love and salvation.

Then follows a beautiful description of what His salvation means in the life of a community or a

nation (9–13). Peace, righteousness, steadfast love
and faithfulness blend together (10–11), and, as an
added blessing, the harvest will be very good too
(12).

In *Common Worship* this psalm is set for
Christmas Eve. It gives a lovely anticipation of the
blessings Jesus came to bring.

- Pray for your country that the Lord may make it
  a place where truth flourishes and righteousness
  and peace are linked together.

Psalm 86
The insistent prayer of someone
who feels his need is desperate

Incline your ear, O Lord, and answer me,
for I am poor and in misery.

The feature of this psalm is that it is full of petitions. The speaker keeps on asking and asking and
asking. He has certainly got the message of the
teaching Jesus gave centuries later about persist-
ence in prayer, in the parable of the friend at mid-
night (Luke 11:5–8) and the parable of the unjust
judge and the persistent widow (Luke 18:1–7).

The first part (1–7) is a series of petitions. Then

comes a section of praise (8–10) and thanksgiving (12–13), in confident anticipation that his prayer will be answered. But then the speaker returns to his complaint (14) and the psalm ends with more petitions: 'turn ... give strength ... save ... show me' (16–17).

- Pray for people who feel desperate. Think of people you know, or from what you have heard or read, imagine situations which make people feel desperate, and pray for people in such situations.

Psalm 87
A song of Zion, a city for all nations

Glorious things are spoken of you,
Zion, city of our God.

This short psalm, with its staccato phrases, is in praise of Zion, as the home and destiny of all nations. Zion is the city that God chose to found (verse 1). The verses in the middle of the psalm are ambiguous. Do they mean that the people of God, born in Jerusalem, are now scattered and living in many different countries? Or do they mean that these nations, historically enemies of Israel, or like

Ethiopia representative of the edges of the known world, will ultimately find their home in the city of God?

Either way, Zion is a place of refreshment where springs of water gush out of dry rock. This is one of the passages in the Old Testament which lies behind the final vision of the New Testament in Revelation 21 – 22, a vision of the new city of God and of the river of the water of life flowing from it.

This psalm was the inspiration of John Newton's lovely hymn, 'Glorious things of Thee are spoken'.

• Picture in your mind the ultimate city of God, to which the treasures of all nations will be brought to glorify Him and from which will flow the refreshing water of His Spirit. Praise God for His ultimate purposes.

Psalm 88
A cry of despair from someone close to death

My life draws near to the land of death.

More than any other, psalm 88 is an expression of complete despair, without a glimmer of light or hope. In many of the laments, the psalmist remembers what the Lord has done in the past, and finds hope in it, but here there is no mention of it. Nearly all laments end on a note of hope, but in this psalm the speaker sees no future other than death.

Psalm 88 is read on Wednesday in Holy Week in *Common Worship*, and on Good Friday in the *Book of Common Prayer*. By reading it at the time of our Lord's death we are invited to enter into his experience of desolation.

It starts with a cry for help. Then from verse 3 the speaker describes his current experience. He is as good as dead. His reference to his failing eyesight suggests he may be dying of diabetes. Then comes his prayer for deliverance. He bases his appeal on the argument that the Lord has no contact with the dead. 'If you do not act now, you will not be able to take action later on.' (The psalm offers a typical Old Testament view of life after death as a shadowy existence cut off from the presence of God.) The prayer ends without even a spark of hope.

This psalm is a profound expression of trust in the Lord. Even the darkest depths of despair, where there is no hope at all, can be brought to Him. There is no pretence here, no stiff upper lip hiding the blackness within. The psalm has a very keen awareness of God. The words 'you' or 'your' appear in nearly every verse. Even the worst of our feelings are to be addressed to Him.

- Pray for those who are deeply depressed, those who are in despair and can find no hope at all, those thinking of suicide. Pray that they may be able to express their true feelings to the Lord in prayer, and may begin to experience the light that He gives. Pray for the Samaritans and for all those who are close to people considering suicide.

Psalm 89
The cry of a people
who have seen their country devastated

Although the opening part of the psalm is a hymn of praise (verses 1–18), at its heart it is a communal lament, the cry of a people who have been defeated in battle and seen their country ruined (38–45).

Verses 1–18

My song shall be always of the loving kindness of the Lord;
with my mouth I will proclaim your faithfulness throughout all generations.

From the present disastrous situation the psalmist looks back to the past and to the Lord's goodness to Israel. In a hymn of praise (1–18) God's power

and faithfulness are extolled in lyrical language.
This part of the psalm could stand on its own as a
separate psalm. There is no hint here of the present
situation. The song is full of the goodness of the
Lord. The description makes the contrast with
Israel's current situation all the more acute. The
references to the Lord's covenant (3–4), to his
power (8–13), and to his justice and faithfulness
(14–16), all build up the argument, pressing the
Lord to take action.

- Is your community happy, comfortable, enjoying
  the gifts of the Lord? Or is life for most people a
  constant wearying struggle? Whichever it is,
  pray for those whose life experience contrasts
  with yours.

Verses 19–51

You have cast off and rejected your anointed;
you have shown fierce anger against him.

Verses 19–37 set out the terms of the permanent
covenant the Lord has established with David and
his descendants. The emphasis is that the Lord's
promise is 'for ever'. If David's descendants fail to
keep the covenant, they will face penalties but the
Lord will not abandon them. This emphasis is

intended to press the Lord to keep His promises. (These promises are set out in 2 Samuel 7: 8–16.)

In verses 38–45 comes the heart of the psalm, the lament, the protest to the Lord. The King has been defeated in battle. It seems the Lord has forgotten his covenant. The repeated 'I' of the Lord's promises given in the covenant turns to the reproachful 'you' of the complaint.

The psalm ends with a prayer that the Lord will remember his promises and be faithful to David's descendants (46–51). The argument is pressed home with the double 'remember' (47 and 50), and with a piteous presentation of the people's distress.

The final verse is a short doxology which marks the end of Book III of the psalms.

- Think of countries which have been ruined by war, with many buildings destroyed, road and rail links broken – for example, Zaire or Afghanistan. Pray for the people of those countries in their sense of desolation.

> The Psalms are the poetry of the reign of the Lord.
>
> James B. Mays

Book Four
Psalms 90 – 106

Psalm 90
Out of adversity, a prayer for wisdom

*So teach us to number our days
that we may apply our hearts to wisdom.*

Sometimes the experience of adversity has the effect of moving people to reflect deeply on the meaning of life. The person who has gone through suffering emerges as a deeper person. This magnificent psalm can be seen as an example of this.

The first part of the psalm (verses 1–11) is a meditative reflection. It starts with an acknowledgement that the Lord is the speaker's home and refuge (1–2). Then comes a reflection on the transitoriness of human life in comparison with the eternity of God (3–11). The speaker's serenity in the face of human mortality and death is based on the security that comes from knowing God is eternal.

The psalm then speaks of God's displeasure and anger, but the reference to sins show the speaker recognises God's indignation is justified (7–8).

In verse 12 comes the heart and focus of the psalm – a prayer for wisdom, that is, an understanding of God's purposes that leads to a life that is lived in alignment with them.

Then follows a vigorous complaint, calling on the Lord not to delay but to take action (13–15). Trust in God does not lead to passive acceptance. Verse 17 is perhaps an unexpected ending. Its reference to 'the work of our hands' emphasises the value of human achievement, in spite of our brief life-span.

Psalm 90 provides the inspiration and model for Isaac Watts' well-loved hymn, 'O God our help in ages past'.

- Imagine some point in the future when your life has come to an end. Look back on your present life from that point. Are you satisfied with the way you are living? Pray for wisdom, that you may make a sound estimate of your present way of life, and be able to make any changes that may be appropriate.

Psalm 91
A song of trust in the Lord's protection

*Whoever dwells in the shelter of the Most High
and abides under the shadow of the Almighty.*

This psalm conveys a mood of quiet confidence in
the Lord who protects us from the greatest dangers
we face and from the things we fear most – the sudden attack at night (verse 5), the unexpected accident which comes like an arrow out of the blue (5),
the deadly illness that strikes us without warning
(6).

The rest of the psalm develops this theme. The
form in which it is set, an address from one person
to another, suggests it may have been used as a
blessing. In the final section (14–16), it is the Lord
who is speaking, promising his protection.

- Think about things that you fear most for yourself and for those closest to you, and in a prayer
  claim the protection that the Lord has promised.

Psalm 92
A song of thanksgiving

It is a good thing to give thanks to the Lord.

This psalm is full of gladness and gratitude to the Lord for his goodness. It starts with a short hymn of thanksgiving and praise (verses 1–4). Then the psalmist ponders the mystery and wonder of God (5–9). The immediate cause of thanksgiving is explained: the Lord has vindicated the speaker, and the enemies that threatened have been overthrown (10–11), though no details are given. The psalmist ends with a statement of faith that is reminiscent of psalm 1 (12–15).

- Think about the things that you most value in life and thank God for them.

A collection of songs of the Kingdom of God

Psalms 93 and 95 – 99 form a small collection of psalms celebrating the coming of the Kingdom of God. They offer us a vision of a world in which God's reign is fully realised. It is a vision that will nourish our hope and raise our spirits when we face set back or disaster. It is a vision which provides the seeds from which sprang Jesus' good news of the Kingdom. It may be helpful to read the section 'Songs of the Kingdom of God' in Part One (pages 24–26).

Psalm 93
A hymn to the Lord the King

The Lord is King.

The psalm starts with an announcement, a proclamation: 'The Lord is King'. That is the key statement from which everything else is derived. His reign is established, though it still faces opposition and conflict.

Floods are one of the most powerful and destructive of natural disasters. In the Bible the force and the turbulence of floodwaters and of the sea are images of the forces of evil rising up in opposition to the reign of God. The psalm celebrates the Lord's strength. He is unmoved by the power of the forces ranged against Him.

- Picture in your mind the waves of the sea breaking against a rock with all their force, day after day, year after year, but the rock remains unmoved. Hold this picture in your mind, and thank God that He is our rock.

Psalm 94
A cry to the Lord to take action
as judge of those who oppress His people

Rise up, O judge of the earth;
give the arrogant their just deserts.

This psalm is a cry for justice, an appeal for help based on the argument that evil people must not be allowed to go on triumphing (verse 3). The complaint (4–7) describes what such people are now doing to the weak and vulnerable. Then follows an appeal to people to understand the ways of the Lord (8–15). Then, remembering what the Lord has done in the past, the psalmist ends with an expression of confidence and trust (17–23).

- Pray for people who are suffering the kinds of things described in verses 4–6: repeated verbal abuse, threats of violence and intimidation, damage to their homes, beatings, death threats to themselves or their families, kidnapping, murder.

Psalm 95
A song of joy to the Lord, to a great King

*O come let us sing to the Lord,
let us heartily rejoice in the rock of our
salvation.*

Psalm 95 has been known to generations of Anglicans as the opening canticle in Morning Prayer, the Venite (from the Latin for 'O come'). It makes a fine introduction to worship, calling on people to sing to give expression to their joy (verses 1–2).

The opening word of verse 3, 'for', introduces the reason for this joy and praise: 'He is a great God, and a great King above all gods'. The basis for His kingship is set out. He created the world (3–5). It is shaped and held by Him. Then the call to worship is repeated, but now it is more solemn and reverent (6–7).

The last part of the psalm is a warning against a failure to listen and respond to the Lord's guidance. The Lord himself is the speaker in verses 8–11. The idea that worship without obedience is displeasing to God is central to the Old Testament and is a repeated theme in the prophets. These verses are quoted in the New Testament in the Letter to the Hebrews, chapters 3 and 4.

- Give thanks to God that the whole world is His, from the peaks of the highest mountains to the troughs of the sea-bed. Pray for the coming of His Kingdom, that His will be done on earth as in heaven.

Psalm 96
A song of the coming Kingdom of God

Let the heavens rejoice and let the earth be glad ...
for (the Lord) comes, he comes to judge the earth.

This psalm calls on all peoples, the whole world, to sing a *new* song in praise of the Lord. The message is to be told and declared to all nations and peoples (verse 3). Heaven and earth, human beings and the whole physical creation are called on to rejoice.

The build-up of repeated words – 'sing ... sing ... sing ... ascribe ... ascribe ... ascribe ... he is coming ... he is coming' – creates an atmosphere of growing excitement. The Lord is coming to judge the earth, that is, He is coming to protect the rightful claims of the poor and weak, and to bring to an end the misuse of power by the rich and influential. The judgement of the Lord is only to be feared by those who have abused their power. The helpless and the vulnerable are delighted at the prospect of His judgement.

- Pray for justice between nations, in the trading relationships between the rich and powerful nations and poor and weak ones, for justice for the poorest countries which are heavily in debt.

Psalm 97
A song of the universal reign of God

The Lord is king! Let the earth rejoice;
let the multitude of the isles be glad!

Like psalms 93 and 99, this psalm opens with a proclamation, 'The Lord is King!' That is cause for rejoicing throughout the world (verse 1). The next section (2–6) weaves together the qualities of His reign, righteousness and justice, with a vivid description of power, using the metaphor of a thunderstorm.

Then the psalm brings out the contrasting reactions to the Lord's reign (7–9). For idol worshippers it means shame and humiliation, but those who serve Him are delighted with His judgements.

His rule is an especial joy to those who are upright and hate evil (10–12).

- Remember Prisoners of Conscience, those imprisoned for their religious and political beliefs who have never advocated or practised violence. Pray for them as light dawns bringing a new day, with the fear of maltreatment or torture and the hope of release.

Psalm 98
A song of the coming Kingdom of God

*In righteousness shall he judge the world,
and the peoples with equity.*

Like psalm 96, this psalm starts by calling on people to sing a new song, and ends with the whole physical universe rejoicing at the coming of the Lord.

The emphasis of the opening verses is on the Lord's victory over all the forces in the world that oppose Him and His reign. The Hebrew word can be translated 'victory' or 'salvation'. It appears three times in the opening verses. When you are facing an enemy determined to defeat you and destroy you the only way to be saved is to win the battle. The Lord's victory is a cause for rejoicing for the whole world.

The whole earth is called to praise the Lord in joyful song, and the physical universe, sea and hills, is invited to join in. The reason for this joy and praise is given in the final verse: 'The Lord is coming to establish a rule of justice'.

- Pray for people who at present are not receiving justice: because mistakes have been made, perhaps, or because powerful people are manipulating the processes of the law. Pray that they may receive justice and catch a glimpse of God's Kingdom.

Psalm 99
A hymn of praise to the Lord the King

The Lord is King; let the peoples tremble.

This psalm, like psalms 93 and 97, opens with a proclamation: 'The Lord is King', but this time the response to the announcement is reverence and awe. Peoples tremble and the earth quakes (verse 1). He rules all nations (2) and establishes justice (4). The refrain in verses 5 and 9 calls on us to exalt and worship Him.

The second part of the psalm praises Him as the God who answered His people when they called on Him from slavery in Egypt. The pillar of cloud (Exodus 13:21 etc.) and the giving of the Law (Exodus 20) make it clear this is referring to the Exodus. The closing verses are a reminder that mercy and forgiveness are an essential part of God's commitment.

• If your situation allows, kneel and bow your head. Remember that you are in the presence of God, who is holy and awesome, as powerful as an earthquake, as searing as lightning.

Psalm 100
A song of thankful praise

Enter His gates with thanksgiving
and His courts with praise.

This short hymn of praise, calling on the whole earth to praise the Lord, forms a doxology (a final shout of praise) to the collection of hymns on the kingly rule of God. Often called the Jubilate, it is traditionally sung at Mattins, the morning service of the Church. It is full of joy and gladness.

The hymn 'All people that on earth do dwell',

usually sung to the tune 'The Old Hundredth' is a metrical version of this psalm.

- Think of the thing for which you are most grateful to God and thank Him for it. Think of the thing for which you most wish to praise God and praise Him for it.

Psalm 101
A king's pledge to rule justly

I will sing of faithfulness and justice.

This psalm has the character of an act of dedication or a pledge. It has been suggested that it was a declaration the King of Judah had to make at his enthronement.

The first half of the psalm is about personal behaviour. It has both positive statements about living with integrity or purity of heart, and also the repudiation of what it is evil or unfaithful.

The second half is the statement of a head of government who pledges himself not to employ dishonest or deceitful people in his administration. Those who privately denigrate rivals will not be tolerated. In the final verses he pledges that in his role as judge he will dispense justice each day.

• Pray for the most senior members of the government of your country, that they may be wise in making appointments, perceptive in assessing people's true character and firm in rejecting those who are deceitful or dishonest.

Psalm 102
The cry of someone who is mourning and is seriously ill

My days fade away like a shadow,
and I am withered like grass.

One of the Seven Psalms, 102 is a very personal statement, with a vivid description of the speaker's experience, but with a section that links it with the corporate experience of the people of Israel.

It starts with a cry for help. There follows the lament, a strong expression of what life is like for the speaker. The lament begins and ends with a thought about the fleeting nature of life which expresses the speaker's sense of the nearness of death. 'My days are consumed in smoke ... my days fade away like a shadow.' The account contains many symptoms of bereavement:

days pass away like smoke – life feels unreal,
  pointless
withered like grass – everything seems flat, dry
forget to eat bread – no appetite
like an owl that haunts the ruins – feeling of
  desolation, isolation
I keep watch/lie awake – finds it difficult to get to
  sleep

The next section (verses 12–22 in the Bible; 13–23
in *Common Worship*) feels like a later addition. It
links the personal experience of the first section
with the communal or national experience of
Israel. It expresses the pain felt over the destruction
of Jerusalem and the deportation of many people
into exile in Babylon.

If you find it hard to share its feeling, try to imagine seeing your home town flattened by bombing
and being carried off and dumped down in a
refugee camp in a foreign country.

Then in the final section the individual prayer is
resumed. It contrasts God's everlastingness with
the speaker's sense that death is near. It focuses on
God's creative activity, but emphasises what He
has created will also perish. For someone nearing
death, security can only be found in God. The final
verse links the continuation of people through the
generations with God's enduring presence.

- In silence remember all those who have been bereaved, especially those whose loss has been sudden or premature, whether through illness or accident or violent attack. Bring them in their grief and pain into the presence of God. Then remember all those who have seen their homes destroyed and are now forced to live in refugee camps or as asylum seekers in a foreign country, and pray for them.

Psalm 103
A hymn of praise to the generous Lord

Bless the Lord, O my soul,
and all that is within me, bless His holy name.

(NRSV)

This is a magnificent hymn of praise. To many English-speaking Christians it is best known through the much-loved hymn that it inspired, 'Praise, my soul, the King of heaven' by H. F. Lyte.

As many psalms of praise do, it starts with a summons, a call to praise. At first the opening can seem slightly odd. The speaker is addressing herself: 'Bless the Lord, O my soul.' When one becomes familiar with the psalm, one no longer notices this.

The first two verses illustrate a feature of

Hebrew poetry. The second line of verse one repeats the first line, saying the same thing but in different words. The second line of verse two complements the first line, giving new meaning to it.

These opening verses give one of the key themes of the psalm: 'Do not forget'. *Remembering* is a key theme in the Bible and in the spirituality of both Judaism and Christianity. For Judaism this is focused in the Passover meal, celebrated each year to remember how God set free His people from slavery in Egypt and formed them into a nation so that they might serve Him.

For Christians it comes to the fore in the service of Holy Communion – the Eucharist, the Lord's Supper. At the Last Supper, on the night before his death, Jesus gave His disciples instructions to eat bread and to drink wine, '*in remembrance of me*'. Each time we do this we remember that His body was given for us and His blood shed for us for the forgiveness of our sins.

Remembering what has been done for us leads us to appreciate it and to value it. Appreciation is the basis for that spirit of gratitude which is close to the heart of Christian spirituality.

By remembering what has happened in the past, we bring it into the present so that it shapes our lives today.

Verses 3–5 give the grounds for which we are to

praise God. Six verbs describe what the Lord has done. They are echoed in the hymn by the magnificent lines

Ransomed, healed, restored, forgiven,
Who like me his praise should sing.

They provide a wonderful reminder of the many different ways in which God has affected our lives.

Then in verses 6–7 the psalm moves on to a new theme with its reference to Moses. It speaks about the events of the Exodus. It may perhaps seem surprising to introduce this theme at this point, but it shows the way in which the psalmist thinks. For him the Exodus, the escape from slavery in Egypt, is the foundation of his faith. It is the action of the Lord that provides the basis for understanding His character and His purpose for the world. It is the supreme example of His saving power.

Verses 8–18 form the main body of the psalm. They describe the Lord's goodness in relation to two aspects of human life, human failure and human finitude. The key word is 'mercy', which recurs four times, in verses 4, 8, 11 and 17. (Some translations use different words such as 'steadfast love', but it is the same word in the original Hebrew of the psalm.)

Verses 8–13 develop the theme of verse 3a, 'who

forgives all your iniquity'. They speak about the Lord's goodness in relation to human failure. His fundamental response is one of mercy. He is a God who forgives. But His mercy does not abolish His anger. The Lord's anger is His reaction to everything that threatens and constricts life. It results in His judgement on those things which frustrate his purposes of love for the world.

His mercy does not abolish His anger but limits it. The relationship between them is beautifully caught by a verse in another psalm:

> His anger is but for a moment;
> his mercy is for a lifetime.

(Psalm 30:5)

In the hymn this idea is expressed in the lovely line, 'Slow to chide, and swift to bless'.

Verses 14–18 develop the theme of verse 3b, 'who heals all your diseases'. As human life is restricted by sin, so it is cut short by death. His awareness of our frailty moves Him to compassion, just as a human father is moved to compassion by the weakness and vulnerability of his little children. Human frailty is compared to that of a flower, beautiful but so vulnerable. It blooms, but when the hot desert wind blows, it dies within a few hours. (For many years I imagined the writer was speaking about a cold wind because I thought of the effects of a late frost on the blossom of an apple tree and on plants that flower early, but in the Holy Land the hot wind is a much greater problem than the cold one.) There are echoes of this passage in the hymn,

Father-like, he tends and spares us;
Well our feeble frame he knows.

The line in the psalm, 'He remembers that we are dust', has echoes in the funeral service: 'Ashes to ashes, dust to dust'. Verses from psalm 103 are often read in the funeral service.

The psalm ends as it began, with a summons, a call to praise, but now it is not addressed simply to an individual, but all the angels and hosts of heaven are caught up in praising the Lord. The final line of the psalm repeats the first line, but now as part of a great chorus.

• Read the first two verses again, and remember some of the many benefits and blessings the Lord has given you. Remember and be grateful.

Psalm 104
A hymn of praise to the Lord,
the Creator of the universe

O Lord, how manifold are your works!
In wisdom you have made them all.

Verses 1–23 (1–25 in *Common Worship*)

This song of creation opens and closes with the same words as psalm 103. It is a lyrical and exuberant hymn, full of wonder at the world God has made.

The first section portrays the Lord as the sovereign Creator, with an imaginative pictorial description, featuring Him as a king going out in a chariot to lay the foundations of the earth.

The second section looks with wonder at the provision the Lord makes for all His creatures – water, food, habitat and the ordering of night and day. Human beings are included among the creatures for whom the Lord provides, though they are mentioned as 'the last word'.

- Give thanks for this beautiful and amazing world which the Lord has entrusted to us. Pray that we may be responsible in caring for it, refraining from action that will damage it through pollution, destruction of species, or desertification.

Verses 24–35 (26–37 in *Common Worship*)

The third section of this hymn of praise starts with an expression of amazement at how many different creatures the Lord has made. As well as those on the land already mentioned, there are all those in the sea. And all of them depend on Him for food and for life itself.

The last section is the psalmist's response to the wonder of creation. It is a response of prayer, a prayer that recognises the joy the Lord Himself finds in His creation. It is also a commitment to life-long praise.

The final verse strikes a note that jars on our ears. The wicked are to be excluded. But this is because they spoil the Lord's creation because they do not live in accordance with His purposes.

The last word of the psalm is 'Hallelujah' or 'Praise the Lord', the first 'Hallelujah' in the Book of Psalms. (But some commentators think this word is really the first word of psalm 105.)

Psalm 104 is set for Pentecost (Whit Sunday) in both the *Book of Common Prayer* and *Common Worship*. At first sight it is a strange choice, since it is a hymn of creation, while Pentecost celebrates the gift of the Holy Spirit. The key is found in verse 30 (32 in *Common Worship*). It speaks of the Lord sending forth His Spirit or His breath (the same word in Hebrew), and renewing the face of the earth.

This psalm was the inspiration of Robert Grant's hymn 'O worship the King all glorious above'.

• See the first section above.

Psalm 105
A song of praise to the Lord, recounting Israel's history

Seek the Lord and his strength,
seek his face continually.
Remember the marvels He has done.

Verses 1–22

This psalm and the next form a pair of psalms which complete Book IV of the Psalms. They both begin and end with 'Hallelujah' - 'Praise the Lord'. They both tell the story of Israel's history, but from contrasting points of view. This psalm focuses on the Lord's unfailing care and provision for Israel. The next one emphasises Israel's repeated unfaithfulness.

The psalm begins by calling people to praise the Lord and to remember what He has done (verses 1–5). The story starts with Abraham and the covenant God made with him, promising him the land of Canaan (Genesis 15:18–20). (For 'Abraham' see the Glossary, page 46.) It then goes on to the story of Joseph, a wonderful story told in Genesis 37 and 39 – 48. (For 'Joseph' see the Glossary, page 50.)

• Look back and see if you can find examples of God's care and provision in your life, in the life of your parents or grandparents, in the history of your country or nation. Remember them and give thanks to Him.

Verses 23–45

The second part of the psalm tells the story of the Exodus (see the Glossary, page 49). It recounts how the people of Israel escaped from slavery in Egypt and came to take possession of the land promised to Abraham (verses 42–44). All the way through the emphasis is on the Lord's action, His protection, His provision. The final verse highlights His purpose. He has kept His promise and covenant (42). Now Israel is to keep its side of the covenant, and be a people whose way of life is in accordance with His principles (45).

• See verses 1–22 above.

Psalm 106
A song of thanksgiving for the Lord's faithfulness
to His unfaithful people

We have sinned like our forebears.

Verses 1–23

The second of a pair of psalms (see the comments on psalm 105), this psalm emphasises how difficult and stubborn the people of Israel were. It starts by thanking the Lord that He is always faithful (verse 1) and with a prayer (4).

It then tells the story of the Exodus from Egypt, and the journey through the wilderness of Sinai (see the Glossary, page 54), referring to many of the events that come in the Book of Exodus. The story of the golden calf outlined in verses 19–23 is told in Exodus 32. Perhaps the key words are 'they forgot' (13, 21).

- Look back over the past year to think if there have been times when you have forgotten what God has done for you, when you have been ungrateful and difficult. Confess these to Him, and receive His forgiveness.

Verses 24–end

The account of the Israelites' journey through the wilderness continues. On their first approach to the Promised Land, fear of what they might encounter made them lose confidence in God. They refused to enter it (verse 24). The full story is in the Book of Numbers, chapters 13 – 14. The events referred to in verses 28–31 are described in Numbers 25. The last part of the psalm (35–47 *Common Prayer*; 35–46 Bible) describes the people of Israel living in the land of Canaan and being led astray by the other nations living there.

The story ends by emphasising God's mercy. He remembers His covenant with Israel, so that their captors have pity on them.

The psalm ends with a prayer, perhaps from during or after the Exile, that Israel may be saved and gathered together. The last verse is the doxology at the end of Book IV of the Psalms.

• See verses 1–23 above.

Book Five
Psalms 107 – 150

Psalm 107
A song of thanksgiving
that the exiles have come home

Let them give thanks to the Lord for His
goodness
and the wonders He does for His children.

Verses 1–22

The psalm starts by giving thanks to the Lord that He has gathered people together, bringing the exiles from Babylon and other countries back to their own land (verses 1–3).

Then follow four stanzas, each beginning in a similar way and ending with a refrain. They describe the experience of the exiles, and the difficulties from which they have been rescued. First there are those who were lost in the desert and nearly died of hunger and thirst (4–9). Then there are those who were put in prison (10–16), though this was a judgement on the way they had rejected God's guidance.

The third stanza is about those who were sick (17–22). The first word in the Hebrew is 'Fools', emphasising that, like the person who experiments with drugs today, they brought trouble on themselves.

• Pray for those who are weakened by hunger and thirst, especially those whose lives are threatened by starvation. Pray for those who are being held hostage, and for all who are in prison, whether this is a fair sentence for what they have done or they are unjustly held, e.g. Prisoners of Conscience. Pray for those who are experimenting with drugs or those addicted to them, that they may be rescued from this danger.

Verses 23–43

The fourth stanza focuses on those who have had to travel to Jerusalem by sea and have been caught in a violent storm (verses 23–32). They have survived because the Lord calmed the storm. (This reminds Christians of the time when Jesus stilled the storm on the Sea of Galilee, Luke 8:22–25.)

The last part of the psalm is a hymn of praise to the Lord who brings about these reversals of fortune (33–41). He settles the hungry in a fertile land (36–38), just as He did to the people of Israel in the Promised Land. By Him princes are brought low but the poor are raised up out of their misery.

The final verse encourages us to think about these things. Remembering and considering is a key theme in the spirituality of the psalms.

• Remember times in your life when something that seemed to be disastrous turned out well, when there was a complete change for the better, and thank God for these. Pray for all those who are travelling by land, sea or air, and are in danger.

Psalm 108
A song of prayer for victory in battle

O grant us your help against the enemy,
for earthly help is in vain.

This psalm starts as a song of thanksgiving. (The first five verses are also in psalm 57:7–11; 8–12 in *Common Worship*.) It is only when you get to the second part that you realise this is giving thanks in advance, in anticipation.

It then becomes a prayer for deliverance and victory (verses 6, 12–13). (The same prayer is also in psalm 60:5–12.) After a short prayer (6) there is an oracle (7–9), a statement made in God's name, perhaps by a Temple official. God rules over the land of Israel, the places named in verses 7–8. Ephraim and Judah, tribes of Israel, have the honour of being called God's helmet and sceptre. Israel's traditional enemies in verse 9 are given menial positions.

The psalm ends with a prayer for help in the coming battle (10–12) and an expression of confidence of victory through God's power.

- Over and over again in recent years nations and communities have had to suffer attack from powerful neighbours – in southern Sudan and East Timor, Kurds in Iraq and Albanians in Kosovo. Pray for those who find themselves threatened by powerful enemies.

Psalm 109
A cry for deliverance from vicious enemies

Let them curse, but you O Lord will bless.

(NRSV)

This is a difficult psalm to make sense of. At the centre of it is a long and appalling curse (verses 5–18 *Common Worship*; 6–19 Bible). The psalmist's enemies have put a curse on him (27 *Common Worship*; 28 Bible). To bring home to the Lord what a terrible situation he is in, he repeats the terrible curse that has been put on him. His response (19, 28 *Common Worship*; 20, 29 Bible) is mild in comparison.

Any understanding of this psalm requires an appreciation of the psalmist's situation, the intense hated that he is facing, the lies that are being spread about him, and his own struggle to love the people who are treating him like this and to pray for them (2–4 *Common Worship*; 2–5 Bible).

He appeals to the Lord (20–26 *Common Worship*; 21–27 Bible), both on the grounds of his steadfast love and mercy (see 'Mercy' in the Glossary, page 52), and also on the grounds of his own weakness and the pain he is suffering. He asks for justice, that those who have put a curse on him may taste their own medicine (19 *Common Worship*; 20 Bible).

It is a very uncomfortable psalm. It is truthful in that it is honest and open in speaking to the Lord about the bitterness and hatred there is in the world, and which is sometimes experienced. It is faithful in placing the matter in the Lord's hands. But the hatred itself is left unresolved.

- Is there anyone you hate or feel very bitter towards? Is there anyone you feel hates you? Do you know someone who hates or is hated? Imagine the hatred felt by people who have suffered very greatly in 'ethnic cleansing', gang rapes or other terrible crimes. Bring this hatred to the Lord.

Psalm 110
A psalm for the enthronement of a King

The Lord said to my lord, 'Sit at my right hand.'

The psalm reads like one that has been composed for the enthronement of a King. It is addressed to the King, and consists of two statements in a style typical of the prophets. They begin, 'The Lord says' (verse 1) and 'The Lord has sworn' (4). He is invited to sit at the right hand of the Lord, a position of authority and power. He is to be a priest, one who comes to God on behalf of his people. He will be a priest like Melchizedeh, whose name means 'King of justice'. He is promised victory in battle.

This psalm is frequently quoted or referred to in the New Testament – in the Gospels, in the Acts of the Apostles, in the letters of St Paul and the letter to the Hebrews. The apostles see verse 1 as referring to Jesus, the Messiah, the Christ, who is descended from David and has been raised by God from the dead and exalted to His right hand (e.g. Acts 2:32–36). So this is naturally a psalm for Ascension Day.

- Give thanks to God that He has raised Jesus from the dead and given Him authority and power. Ponder what that means for the life of the world, its tensions, its violence, its injustice.

Psalm 111
A hymn to the Lord for His great works

*The works of the Lord are great,
sought out by all who delight in them.*

Psalms 111 and 112 are a pair. Both begin with 'Hallelujah' - 'Praise the Lord'. Both are acrostics, with twenty-two lines beginning with successive letters of the Hebrew alphabet. The alphabet provides the structure rather than any progress or development of thought.

The key theme is the goodness of God shown in His works. These are wonderful and powerful (verses 4, 6), but there is also the steady, faithful provision of food each day (5). The reassuring stability of verses 7–8 is matched by the awesome activity of verse 9. The final verse, with its reference to 'the fear of the Lord', meaning 'reverence' and 'awe', looks forward to the next psalm.

• Praise the Lord for His steady, regular provision for our needs. Ponder which works of the Lord you find awesome, and praise Him for them.

Psalm 112
A wisdom psalm: the happiness of those who delight in the Lord's way of life

Blessed are those who fear the Lord,
and have great delight in his commandments.

Where psalm 111 focused on the activity of the Lord, psalm 112 focuses on the way of life of those who live the Lord's way. These are people who are generous with what they have, willing to lend, and fair in business dealings (verse 5). They also give freely to those in need (9). They sound very nice people, and the psalms call them 'the righteous'.

They will enjoy prosperity (4). They live without worrying about things because they trust the Lord (7). Just to make the point absolutely clear, the psalmist adds a final verse about people who are not like that. Those who are not generous to the poor and fair in their dealings end up angry and resentful at the happiness of those who are.

- Read verses 4–9 again. Pray for yourself, for the members of your local church, for the people of God throughout the world, that we may live in the way these verses describe.

Psalms 113 – 118: Passover Psalms

Psalms 113 – 118 form the 'Egyptian Hallel' or 'Egyptian Praise' in Jewish worship. They are sung to praise God for rescuing the people of Israel from slavery in Egypt. Jewish people see this escape or 'Exodus' from Egypt as the foundation event by which they become a nation. The events surrounding their escape are described in the Book of Exodus 11 – 15.

The Passover festival each year is still celebrated by Jewish people to commemorate this Exodus, as it was in the time of Jesus. It centres on a gathering in the evening which is both a family or communal meal and an act of worship. These six psalms are sung, the first two before the meal, the other four after it.

It was the Passover meal which Jesus celebrated with his disciples on the night that he was arrested and condemned to death. These psalms were probably 'the hymn' which they sang at the end of the evening before they went out to the Mount of Olives and to the Garden of Gethsemane (see Mark 14:26).

The psalms were collected together centuries before Christ. At that time people had no hope of the resurrection. This makes it some task to choose psalms to say or sing at Easter, when Christians celebrate the resurrection of Jesus Christ from the dead. These Passover psalms are linked with the time of Jesus' death and resurrection. From them two victory songs are chosen for Easter, for the theme of victory over death is a key aspect of the resurrection. St Paul ends his teaching on the resurrection of Christ:

Death has been swallowed up in victory;
thanks be to God who gives us the victory through our Lord Jesus Christ.

(1 Corinthians 15:54, 57)

Psalm 113
A hymn of praise to the Lord
who turns situations upside down

*Who is like the Lord our God that has his
throne so high? ...
He raises the poor from the dust and lifts the
needy from the ashes.*

This psalm starts with a sweeping summons to
praise that embraces all time (verse 2) and all places
(3–4). The grounds for praise lies in the contrast
between the loftiness of the Lord's throne and the
lowliness of the people for whom He takes action
(5–7). He is the Lord who turns situations upside
down, raising up those who only survive by scavenging on rubbish tips. But the supreme example of
this turning upside down is that the barren give
birth. Here are echoes of the Song of Hannah in 1
Samuel 2 and of the Magnificat in Luke's Gospel
2:47–55. Underlying it all is the memory of how the
Lord transformed the situation of a rabble of slaves
by enabling them to escape from Egypt.

• Pray for those who only survive by scavenging
  on rubbish tips. Pray for those for whom child-
  lessness is heart-breaking. Pray that the Lord
  may transform their situations.

Psalm 114
A victory song, celebrating God's intervention to rescue His people

When Israel came out of Egypt,
the house of Jacob from a people of a strange
tongue.

This psalm is set for Easter Day in *Common Worship*, as it is in the *Book of Common Prayer*. The deliverance by God from slavery in Egypt that it celebrates is viewed as a precursor of the greater deliverance from the bondage of death that has come through the resurrection of Jesus Christ from the dead. (See the section on Passover Psalms before psalm 113.)

It is a song sung to celebrate a victory. The first two verses tell the story in a nutshell, from leaving Egypt to settling in the Promised Land where the Lord's sanctuary, Jerusalem, is established. The whole natural world, sea and mountains, are involved (verses 3 and 6). The sea flees in terror at God's power, but the mountains and hills dance with delight. The whole earth, usually so stable and secure, trembles at the awesome power of God (7–8).

This imagery is rather typical of Israel, a people who lived among the hills and valleys, and so saw the hills as being on their side. Their traditional enemies, the Philistines, lived on the coastal plain and so were more familiar with the sea, which the Israelites tended to regard as rather threatening.

- Pray for people who are afraid of dying, for those who have been told they have a fatal illness and do not have long to live, for those who are dying – and for those who are close to them and grieving over them. Pray that they may know the victory over death that God has given us in the resurrection of Jesus Christ.

Psalm 115
A communal song of trust and confidence

The heavens are the heavens of the Lord,
but the earth He has entrusted to human beings.

(Translations combined)

This is the third psalm in the 'Egyptian Hallel' and is usually sung after the meal at the Passover. Its structure suggests it was originally a responsive liturgy, perhaps along these lines:

1–2: *Choir* (perhaps): 'Glory to God alone.'
3–8: *Response*: 'Our God does as He pleases but idols have no life at all.'

9–11: *Choir*: 'Israel, trust in the Lord.'
12–13: *Response*: 'He will bless us.'
14–15: Blessing given by a priest.
16–18: Closing hymn of praise to the Lord.

- Pray for those who are attracted and perhaps captivated by false gods (idols) such as wealth, power, fame, social status, the admiration of others. Pray that they may learn to set their hopes on the one true God.

Psalm 116
A song giving thanks for being saved from death

The snares of death encompassed me.

The feature of this psalm is the speaker's sense of how close she (or he) came to death, and her gratitude to the Lord for saving her. It is a reminder of the terrifying situation the Israelites faced at the Exodus, trapped between the Red Sea ahead of them and the Egyptian army and its chariots pursuing them.

As in many thanksgiving songs, in the first part the speaker tells the story of her experience, the troubles she went through and how the Lord saved her. This leads into an expression of praise.

The second part of the psalm focuses on her fulfilment of her vows, which she will do in public, by offering a thanksgiving sacrifice 'in the presence of all His people'.

• Give thanks with those who have come near to death but have survived and have recovered. Also pray for those who have survived disasters (like the destruction of the World Trade Center in New York) but have to live with continuing fears and a sense of guilt that they have survived when others have died.

Psalm 117
A short hymn of praise

Praise the Lord, all you nations.

The first verse is a call to praise, a comprehensive call in which all nations and peoples are included. The second verse gives the reasons for praise, the Lord's steadfast love and faithfulness. It is a brief summary, which is expanded in other hymns of praise.

• Bring into your mind some picture that conveys the idea of 'all nations' – the world photographed from space, a multi-racial group, the United Nations General Assembly. Hold that in your mind and repeat the first verse.

Psalm 118
A victory song of thanksgiving for survival

They hemmed me in, they hemmed me in on every side,
but the Lord came to my help.

The last of the six psalms that form the 'Egyptian Hallel' in Jewish tradition, this psalm is sung at the Passover after the meal to celebrate the escape of the people of Israel from Egypt. Jesus would have sung it with his disciples at the Last Supper. It may well be 'the hymn' referred to Mark 14:26. It is one of the psalms chosen for Easter Day in *Common Worship*, as it was in the *Book of Common Prayer*. (See the section on Passover Psalms before psalm 113.)

The psalm opens by summoning different groups of people to give thanks (verses 1–4) ('House of Aaron' here means the priests). Then follows the story of what happened. The speaker, surrounded by enemies and under intense pressure, called on the Lord, survived the threats to his life, and was given the victory (5–18).

Though the story is told in the first person singular ('I called to the Lord'), there are hints that the speaker is not a single person but the nation of Israel as a whole. The phrase 'all the nations surrounded me' (10) fits an army better than an individual. Verse 14 is a direct quotation from the victory song in Exodus 15:2, sung when the people of Israel were rescued from the Egyptian army that was chasing them.

This thanksgiving song was perhaps sung by people as they came to the Temple for a festival, because the second part of the song is a responsive liturgy sung on arrival. A group of pilgrims, is met by a priest, perhaps with a choir.

19: Request for admission by the pilgrims.
20: Reply: 'Only the righteous may enter.'
21–22: Response of thanksgiving by the pilgrims: 'God is our salvation.'
23–25: Song of praise, perhaps by a choir.
26–27: A blessing sung as the pilgrims come in.
28: Thanksgiving by those who have entered.
29: Final response: the last verse of the psalm echoes the first.

Verse 22 expresses the idea often found in the Bible, that the Lord turns things upside down by choosing the despised and the rejected for positions of honour. (See, for example, psalm 113.) It is quoted by Jesus in Mark 10:12. Peter in his speech in Acts 4:11 quotes it as a description of Jesus.

The Hebrew word for 'save, O Lord' in verse 25 is Hosanna, which becomes the cry of the crowd accompanying Jesus into Jerusalem on the first Palm Sunday (Mark 11:9).

• Look back to a time in your life when you, or those close to you, were under very great pressure. It may have been physical danger or illness, the pressure to do something wrong, or stress at work or from life's responsibilities. Think of how you emerged from this. Thank the Lord that he helped you through and out of this situation.

Psalm 119
A song of Torah, cherishing the written word of God

Your word is a lantern to my feet
and a light upon my path.

Almost every verse in this very long psalm contains the word 'Law' or a word with a similar meaning – for example, 'commandments', 'testimonies', 'statutes', 'word'.

It is an alphabetical psalm, a *tour de force* in playing with words. Each stanza consists of eight verses all beginning with the same Hebrew letter. The twenty-two letters of the Hebrew alphabet come in succession. By this very orderly structure the psalmist seems to be expressing the sense that it is the Torah, the Law, which gives order and structure to life.

The psalm expresses a spirituality that is based on a deep reverence for Scripture and a devotion to individual texts or sayings. It is not trying to develop a line of thought but is a collection of 176 separate sayings honouring the Torah.

It blends two themes: (1) prayer for deliverance from oppression and suffering, which gives the whole psalm a mood of lament; and (2) prayer to be faithful and obedient to the Lord and His word.

It does not seem a good idea to read large chunks of this psalm consecutively. It is probably better to read one stanza a week over a course of twenty-two weeks, as suggested by *Common Worship* and in the scheme of reading at the end of this book.

- Think of a verse or phrase from the Bible that means a lot to you. (If you cannot think of one, choose one of the Beatitudes in Matthew 5 or John 3:16 or Romans 8:38–39 or 1 Corinthians 13.) Say it over to yourself slowly several times, pondering and savouring its meaning. End by thanking God for it.

Songs of Pilgrimage

Psalms 120 – 134 form a small collection within the Book of Psalms. It is very likely they were originally an independent collection that was later incorporated into the Psalter. Called in Hebrew *ma'a lot*, they are Songs of Pilgrimage. In some versions of the Bible they have the heading, 'A Song of Ascents' – that is, a song to be sung when going up to Jerusalem. One of the features of this small collection is that a high proportion of these psalms are *songs of the community*.

Psalm 120
A cry of pain from someone living in exile

Woe is me, that I must lodge in Meshech,
and dwell among the tents of Kedar.

At first sight this seems a strange choice to start the collection. It is a lament, a cry of distress and pain, addressed to the Lord, pleading with him to take action and to deliver the sufferer.

The cause of the psalmist's pain is that he is living in exile, far from his homeland. Meshech and Kedar (verse 5) are remote regions in Asia Minor and Arabia. He is very conscious of the hostility of those around him, and of the lying and deceitfulness that he frequently experiences. In his distress he cries to the Lord and pleads for deliverance.

We do not know why this psalm is placed first in the collection. One explanation is that it is a reminder to those making a pilgrimage to Jerusalem of their fellow countrymen who live far away and who cannot share in the joy of a visit to their beloved Jerusalem. By saying or singing this psalm we identify ourselves with those who are suffering far away, perhaps under persecution, and express our awareness of their isolation and their pain.

- Imagine what it is like living in exile and unable to return home because one is afraid of being arrested, perhaps tortured. Pray for all those who live in refugee camps or in exile.

Psalm 121
A blessing to be used when setting out on a journey

The Lord shall keep watch over your going out and your coming in.

This psalm is a blessing designed to be used at the start of a journey, such as a pilgrimage to Jerusalem. A pilgrimage was a hazardous venture at a time when the traveller faced the danger of attacks by wild animals or by marauding gangs of robbers, of hunger and thirst, of sunstroke during the heat of the day and of cold at night.

The psalm opens with an expression of trust and confidence in the Lord. He is the one who helps. This leads into a blessing, the promise of protection by day and by night, when setting out in the morning and when arriving at the destination in the evening.

- Pray for all those who are travelling, especially those whose journeys are risky or dangerous and those who are nervous about travelling.

Psalm 122
The pilgrims' song when they reach Jerusalem

And now our feet are standing within your gates, O Jerusalem.

This is a song to be sung on arrival at the city of Jerusalem when the pilgrims reach their destination. They look back to the start of their journey, glad that it was suggested to them that they should join the pilgrimage. They gaze around them at the city, savouring its name, admiring its architecture, thinking of the different groups who make up the whole people of God who look to Jerusalem as their spiritual home. They greet the city by praying for it, and at the heart of their prayer is the request for *shalom* – for peace.

- Pray for the cities of your country, that in spite of the disagreements and clashes that are part of urban life, there may be an underlying peace so that people can live in them free from fear.

Psalm 123
A song of trust

*As the eyes of servants look to the hand of their
master,
or the eyes of a maid to the hand of her mistress,
so our eyes wait upon the Lord our God,
until he have mercy upon us.*

This psalm is a song of trust, an expression of
confidence and trust in the Lord. Perhaps the best
known of all the songs of trust is psalm 23, a very
personal expression of faith. Psalm 123 is a
communal song and it leads into an appeal to the
Lord.

At its heart is the comparison between the
servants watching their master or mistress, and the
speakers looking to the Lord. This gives the psalm
its dominant motif of trust. This profound expression of reliance on the Lord intensifies the plea that
follows.

The second part of the psalm is a short lament,
the cry of people who are suffering contempt and
scorn. They are being humiliated by arrogant
people who look down on them. Their description
of their suffering gives urgency to their plea for
mercy.

- Use the first phrase of the psalm to focus your thoughts on the Lord. If other thoughts intrude, repeat the phrase to focus your attention on him again.

Psalm 124
A shout of joy and thanksgiving for an escape

Blessed be the Lord
who has not given us over to be a prey for their
teeth.

The kernel of this psalm is verse 6 (5 in *Common Worship*): 'Blessed be the Lord' – an exclamation, a shout of praise. It is the cry of joy and thanksgiving of people who have been liberated from impending disaster. This shout of praise is followed by the grounds for praise: 'who has not given us over to be a prey to their teeth', and then by the consequences of the Lord's action: they have escaped.

The opening verses are a reflection on this situation. Looking back they recognise the disaster that might have overwhelmed Israel if it had not been for the Lord's deliverance. In a vivid expression the force of the enemy attack is compared with the raging waters of a river in flood that sweeps people away.

The phrase 'Blessed be the Lord' often occurs in narratives and reports in the historical books of the Bible which tell of God's act of deliverance or help. They are 'narrative praise'. An account is given of what God has done, and the story ends with a cry of praise, 'Blessed be the Lord'.

In another vivid metaphor Israel's release is compared to the escape of a bird from a fowler's snare.

The final verse is probably a liturgical addition, designed to make the psalm appropriate for public worship.

- Think of a time when your country has been faced with potential disaster and has escaped, and thank God for it.

Psalm 125
A song of confidence in the Lord's dependability

Those who trust in the Lord are like Mount Zion,
which cannot be moved, but stands fast for ever.

This psalm is, like psalm 123, a communal song of trust with a concluding prayer. It opens with an expression of confidence in the Lord's reliability.

He makes those who trust in him as steady as a mountain. It ends with a simple petition for his blessing.

- Picture in your mind a mountain or a range of hills. Reflect on their solidity and immovability as a picture of God's trustworthiness and dependability.

Psalm 126
A confident prayer for restoration

Restore again our fortunes, O Lord.

A psalm of the community, psalm 126 is a plea for restoration set within an expression of confident trust. It starts with the memory of deliverance in the past, and looks back to previous experience of the Lord's action on behalf of his people. Their amazement and delight at what He has done finds expression in laughter and joyful shouting. This memory of deliverance probably refers to the return from exile in Babylon in 538 BCE.

In the centre of the psalm, verse 4 (5 in *Common Worship*) is a plea in present distress. The phrase 'Restore our fortunes, O Lord' echoes the similar phrase in the opening verse. Streams that become dry river-beds in summer suddenly fill with water when the autumn rains begin.

The opening verses remember the *past*. The central verse is a plea in the *present*. The closing verses are a confident expectation of *future* restoration.

The whole psalm is a fine example of how God's ancient people held fast to Him in time of distress, finding meaning in their history, even in the worst disasters.

- Pray for your country and for the quality of your corporate life as a nation. Think of those areas where something valuable has been lost over the years, and pray that it may be restored.

Psalm 127
The blessings of family life

Children are a heritage from the Lord.

A substantial section of the Old Testament, which includes the Books of Proverbs and Ecclesiastes, is known as wisdom literature. It sets out in didactic form the accumulated wisdom of the community, the fruit of long reflection by the teachers of the community on its experience over the centuries.

Psalm 127 is an example of such wisdom literature. It emphasises that those who trust in the Lord
have no need to be anxious. A safe home and a
family are the Lord's gift. Perhaps it is because the
pilgrims are far away from home and family and
feeling their absence that this psalm is included in
their pilgrimage songs.

- Thank God for the gift of life, for the parents
  that brought you into the world and the good
  things you have received from them. If you have
  children yourself, thank God for them and for
  the joy and delight you have found in them.

Psalm 128
The blessings of family life

*May you see your children's children
and may there be peace upon Israel.*

This is another wisdom psalm. Its focus is on the
way the Lord blesses those who honour and obey
Him. It is a reminder that it is often in the ordinary
things of life, in marriage and children and meals,
that the Lord's blessing is experienced.

The closing verses widen the horizon from the
family to the whole people of God, represented by

their capital city, Jerusalem. If Jerusalem is prosperous, then the whole people of God are blessed. If Israel enjoys peace, each family can live in peace.

- If you are married, thank God for your spouse and all you have received from him/her. If you are single, pray for married friends, especially any who are facing difficulties. If you have grandchildren, pray that they may experience the peace of Christ.

Psalm 129
A prayer for deliverance from national enemies

The ploughers ploughed upon my back and made their furrows long.

This psalm is a lament of the community, a prayer for deliverance from national enemies. It starts with the memory of survival in the past. The Lord has preserved Israel in the past in spite of all her suffering, even though people have had the scars of whips across their backs (verse 3). It moves on to pray that those who now hate Israel and are oppressing the Lord's people may wither away like the grass that grows out of the beaten earth and dried mud on the roof of a house.

- Pray for nations which have suffered greatly in recent years – Bosnia, Kosovo, the Sudan, El Salvador, Afghanistan perhaps. Pray that people who have been through terrible times may not be bitter.

Psalm 130
A cry of someone who has hit rock bottom

Out of the depths have I cried to you, O Lord;
Lord, hear my voice.

This is one of the most profound and moving of all psalms. Often known by the Latin translation of its opening words, *De Profundis*, it is both a lament and a song of trust. It starts with a cry for help, a call to the Lord from the depths of human suffering. It is the cry of a beggar from nowhere. The speaker is aware of his guilt. He acknowledges he is not qualified to approach the Lord but his unworthiness is overridden by the Lord's mercy. His awareness of this mercy moves him with awe.

This awe leads him to hope. Like a watchman waiting, longing for the relief that daybreak brings, he waits for the Lord. He is as confident that the Lord will act as the watchman is that daylight will eventually come.

The closing verses take this prayer of an individual and widen it out so that it becomes the prayer of the whole people of God. Patient waiting for the Lord is a spiritual quality that all God's people need to learn and practice.

One of the features of this psalm is its awareness of human sinfulness and unworthiness in the presence of the Lord. This gives spiritual depth to the intensity of feeling that is expressed in the opening cry.

Psalm 130 also played an important part in the life of John Wesley. In the spring of 1738 he experienced a time of profound spiritual confusion and depression. On 24 May he attended a service at St Paul's Cathedral where psalm 130 was sung as an anthem. That evening he attended a meeting at Aldersgate Street where he felt his heart 'strangely warmed. I felt I did trust in Christ, Christ alone for salvation.' It was an experience that transformed his life.

- Repeat the verse beginning 'I wait for the Lord' slowly two or three times, pondering on the words. Then just remain quiet, aware of the Lord, waiting for Him. If all sorts of thoughts and feelings rush into your mind, offer them to the Lord, and saying the verse again slowly. End the prayer by saying the last two verses of the psalm.

Psalm 131
A trustful surrender to the Lord

I have quieted and stilled my soul,
like a weaned child on its mother's breast.

Psalm 131 is a song of trust, a simple expression of submission to God's will. It starts, unusually, with three negatives. These opening verses reflect a glad and trusting acceptance of life on the terms that God gives. Verse 2 (3 in *Common Worship* and most Psalters) uses the bold metaphor of a small child to express serenity and well-being. Glad submissive reliance leaves one free of anxiety. In the final verse, which may well be a later addition, intimate statements of personal faith are taken up and used by the whole community.

- Be still and let your heart and mind be quiet. Say the phrase, 'O Israel, trust in the Lord' to focus your thoughts on Him. If and when your thoughts wander, say the phrase again to bring them back to Him.

Psalm 132
A song of Zion

The Lord has sworn an oath to David.

This psalm, which probably originated as part of a liturgy, may well be linked with the pilgrims' visit to the Temple. It starts by calling on the Lord to remember David's determination to provide a sanctuary for the Lord. It recites the story of the finding of the Ark in 2 Samuel 6. Ephrathah is another name for Bethlehem, David's city. Jaar, or Jearim, is Kiriath-Jearim where the Ark had been kept.

The psalm continues with a recital of the Lord's promise to David concerning Jerusalem and the Davidic dynasty. It emphasises the importance of Jerusalem in the faith of Israel, because it is the place the Lord has chosen.

• Think of a place that is particularly significant to you in relation to your faith, a church or cathedral, retreat house or camp-site, or a place associated with a profound spiritual experience. Pray for all those who go there and who worship or work there.

Psalm 133
The joy of living together in unity

*Behold how good and pleasant it is
to dwell together in unity.*

This psalm is a song celebrating one of the joys of life as the Lord's blessing. It starts with an opening affirmation of the goodness of harmony in the family and among the people of God. Two vivid metaphors expand this opening statement. Precious oil speaks of well-being and blessing beyond expectation. It reminds us of the extravagantly generous gift of the woman who anointed Jesus' feet in Luke 7:36–50. Dew is life-giving water in a parched land.

This glad experience of living together in unity is recognised as blessing from the Lord, the hidden source of this well-being. The 'hills of Zion' refer to the hills on which Jerusalem is built. Jerusalem, the centre where tribes of Israel come together, is the place where above all this unity of God's people is experienced. It is the ideal place to sing this psalm.

- Pray for your country that it may experience that profound sense of common purpose and unity that respects and values differences.

Psalm 134
An evening blessing

Come bless the Lord, all you servants of the Lord.

This collection of pilgrimage songs closes with a simple liturgy of blessing. The servants of the Lord are summoned to praise him, and his blessing is pronounced. This may be used as a blessing at nightfall, before going to bed, or on departure from Jerusalem, as the pilgrims leave with the Lord's blessing 'from Zion'.

• Give thanks for all those who will work tonight to keep the essential services of the country running, and for those who will praise God in worship tonight.

Psalm 135
A hymn of praise to the Lord who has chosen Israel

Praise the Lord, for the Lord is good.

The psalm starts by calling people to praise the Lord (verses 1–4). He has chosen Jacob (see the Glossary, page 50). He shows His power, first by His control over nature (5–7) and then by the way He rescued Israel from slavery in Egypt, gave them victory over powerful armies opposing them, and finally gave them the land (8–13). (See 'Exodus' in the Glossary, page 49.) His power contrasts with the complete impotence of the idols that the heathen worship (15–18). The psalm ends as it began, by calling people to praise the Lord.

- Reflect on the blessings which God has given to your nation or country. Praise Him for His goodness.

Psalm 136
A hymn of thanksgiving to the Lord
for His enduring mercy

Give thanks to the Lord, for He is gracious,
for His mercy endures for ever.

This hymn of thanksgiving was probably composed with the intention that a cantor would sing the first line of each verse, and the congregation would sing the second line as a response.

The key word in this response is translated as 'mercy' or 'loving-kindness' or 'steadfast love' in different versions. It refers to the patient, continuing love of God who keeps His covenant with Israel, even though the people of Israel so often ignore Him and go their own way, failing to carry out their responsibilities under the covenant.

After the opening call to give thanks (verses 1–3), the psalm recalls the mighty actions of the Lord. He created the heavens and the earth (4–9). He rescued Israel from slavery in Egypt (10–15), led them through the wilderness, gave them victory in battle so they could enter the land promised to Abraham (16–22). Verses 23–25 sum up what the Lord has done, and the psalm ends with a renewed call to give thanks.

Remembering with gratitude what God has done in the past nourishes and strengthens faith today.

• Think back over the history of the people of God over the past two thousand years. Are there any Christians of the past who have been an inspiration to you? Any hymns or prayers from past centuries you especially value? Remember and give thanks.

Psalm 137
A cry of pain from people in exile – a cry for justice

*By the waters of Babylon we sat down and wept,
when we remembered Zion.*

Jerusalem has been captured by the Babylonian army. All its finest buildings have been destroyed. People have been forcibly deported into exile (see 'Exile' in the Glossary, page 48). They are living by the irrigation canals of the Babylonian plain, a strange place to those used to living in the hills of Judah. To the pain of remembering what has happened to their city is added the humiliation of being taunted by those who defeated them in war (verse

3). It reminds us how Jews in the concentration camp at Treblinka during the Second World War were forced to sing and dance.

An experience like this can easily lead people to give up all hope. But here it leads to defiance, to a renewed determination to preserve the memory of Jerusalem and so maintain the hope of return and renewal (5–6).

Underlying this psalm is the conflict the exiles feel inside themselves. They are clinging on to their belief that the Lord has committed Himself to His city Jerusalem and to His people Israel. But now Jerusalem has been destroyed and they are afraid He has abandoned them and broken His promises, or that He is weak and cannot keep them.

From this inner conflict comes a cry for justice. It starts with an appeal to the Lord as a judge in a court of law (7). Then comes the appeal of the powerless against the immense power for violence of the Babylonian war machine. It is a call for retributive justice, that Babylon may suffer what they have made the people of Judah suffer (8–9).

The language is horrendous, but perhaps only those who suffered as terribly as these Jewish exiles can appreciate the depth of feeling that lies behind an outburst like this. It is important to recognise there is no suggestion in the psalm that the speakers will do it. Rather they are calling on the Lord to take action to restore justice. Those of us who have never suffered such cruelty would be wise to avoid making superficial judgements. (See the section 'Cries for justices: cries for retribution' in Part One, pages 38–45.)

- Pray for those who have suffered this kind of cruelty, in Palestine, in the Sudan, especially those living in enforced exile. Remember the bitter anguish they experience day after day, and the intense anger they have to live with.

Psalm 138
A song of thanksgiving for deliverance from trouble

Though the Lord be high, he watches over the lowly;
as for the proud, he regards them from afar.

The speaker starts by giving thanks (verses 1–2). Then, in a way that is typical of thanksgiving psalms, she refers back to her experience of having her prayer answered (3).

Then the speaker bursts into a hymn of praise, praise inspired by a vision of the Lord's greatness. The most powerful human beings on earth will praise the Lord (4–5). But His true greatness is seen in the way in which, while He is enthroned on high, He still cares for and watches over the lowly (6). This is the vision which inspired the Magnificat, the hymn of praise in Luke 1:46–55.

The closing verses are a statement of faith and trust in the Lord, a trust that is based on the speaker's experiences of being rescued from trouble in the past (7–8).

• Pray for those who are powerful and important in their own society, that they may not become proud or arrogant. Pray for those who have little importance in their own society, that they may know they are important in the sight of God.

Psalm 139
A poem of praise to the Lord
who knows us through and through

I thank you, for I am fearfully and wonderfully made.

This is a remarkable and extraordinary psalm. It is the most profound description of the intimate, personal knowledge that the Lord has of each one of us. Thinking about this moves the psalmist to wonder and praise (verse 14, quoted above; 13 in *Common Worship*).

It is an intensely personal psalm. Almost every verse has both the words 'you' or 'your' and the words 'I' or 'me' or 'my'.

The psalm begins and ends on the theme of the Lord's searching and knowing. It starts with the statement, 'O Lord, you have searched me out and known me' (1), and ends with the prayer:

> Search me out, O God, and know my heart;
> Try me and examine my thoughts.
> See if there is any way of wickedness in me.

(23–24)

Yet it includes an intense expression of hatred. It seems remarkable that someone with so deep a sense of intimacy with God can express such ferocity when speaking of the wicked (19–22). Yet these verses are an integral part of the psalm, as this outline shows.

Verses 1–6 (1–5 in Common Worship): Start with an emphatic *you*, and focus on what *the Lord* is doing. He knows whatever the psalmist says or does, though at the time this feels like being trapped, and the one praying the psalm longs to escape.

Verses 7–12 (6–11 in Common Worship): Centred

on *I* and *full of questions*. The Lord is present wherever the one praying the psalm is. Escape is impossible.

Verses 13–16 (12–16 in Common Worship): Start with an emphatic *you* and focus on what the Lord has done.

Verses 17–22: Centred on *I* and *full of questions* and exclamations.

These are not personal enemies. They are not those who speak maliciously about the psalmist, but those who speak maliciously about God. This is about those who hate God, a prayer for the overthrow of bloodthirsty people (19), whose violence is destroying the world that a just God has created. (If this makes you feel the psalmist is rather smug and complacent, read the section 'Cries for justice: cries for retribution' on pages 38–45 in Part One.)

The psalm ends with a prayer for guidance, to be led in the way everlasting (24).

• Read verses 1–18 again and choose a few phrases to repeat, to help you to ponder on God's knowledge of you. End by praying the last two verses as a prayer.

Psalm 140
A cry for deliverance from very frightening enemies

Protect me from the violent.

Some people live in a situation where there are very frightening people around them threatening them – perhaps people from another community or ethnic group threatening to kill them and rape them and drive them from their homes. The psalmist was one of these. (There are also people who, because of their own inner state, imagine that other, quite innocent, people are trying to poison them or do them harm in some way. We call them paranoid.)

The psalm starts by describing just how violent and how menacing these people are (verses 2–5). The psalmist cries out to the Lord for protection, praying that the violence these people are planning may be turned back upon themselves (4, 7–11).

The psalm ends with an expression of trust and confidence: 'I know that the Lord will bring justice' (12).

- Pray for the protection of those who live in constant fear of violence, that through changed circumstances they may be able to live with a sense of security. Pray for those who suffer paranoid delusions, that through inner healing they may come to live in peace and security.

Psalm 141
A prayer for protection against being led astray

O Lord, I call to you;
come to me quickly.

The psalm starts abruptly. Urgent action is needed. Delay is dangerous. But the danger does not seem to be physical violence. What the psalmist is praying for is that she may be protected from saying and doing what is evil (verses 3–4). Her lips are to be guarded against saying what is bitter and malicious and untrue (3). She prays that her heart may not be attracted to what is evil (4), that she may be protected from being trapped into thinking and behaving in the ways evil people do (9).

• Think if there are times and situations when you need to be protected from saying things that are untrue or damaging to others, when your heart is attracted to doing what is clearly wrong. Pray verse 3 and the first part of verse 4 for yourself, and any others who need your prayers.

Psalm 142
The cry of someone who feels completely isolated

No one cares.

Isolation, and the loneliness that it brings, can be very depressing and painful. This psalm reflects these feelings, with its plaintive cry, 'No one cares for me' (verse 4). No wonder the psalmist complains, and pours out her complaint to the Lord (2).

When it has all been poured out, and He has been told of our trouble, then it is time to recognise that the Lord is our refuge (5). He will be generous and bountiful in His dealings with us (7).

- Pray for those who are feeling lonely, feeling that no one cares for them. (If you are one of them, tell the Lord in your own words what your situation is and how you are feeling about it.) Pray for them and for yourself, that they and you may experience the Lord as generous and bountiful.

Psalm 143
The prayer of someone who is exhausted and near to despair

Enter not into judgement with your servant,
for in your sight shall no one living be
justified.

This is the last of the Seven Psalms, and, as in the others, the psalmist shows an awareness and a sensitivity to his own failings and responsibility. He is aware of being under the judgement of God. This is clearest in verse 2 – one of the sentences in the opening to Morning and Evening Prayer in the *Book of Common Prayer*.

The psalmist gives a desperate picture of his situation – exhausted, crushed, near to despair (verses 3–4). He remembers the Lord's action in the past (5). His desperate need, and his trust in the Lord based on past experience, are the arguments he uses to urge the Lord to take action. To them he adds a prayer for guidance (10) which implies dedication to a life lived in accordance with God's will.

• Use verse 2 as a prayer to lead into a prayer in which you confess to the Lord those things you know you have done wrong, either personally or as a member of a group or community. Claim the promise of Jesus to the paralysed man, 'Your sins are forgiven.'

Psalm 144
The prayer of a King for blessing on his country

Happy are the people who have the Lord for their God.

This psalm is very probably a prayer to be prayed by the King, asking for victory in time of battle (verses 10–12 *Common Worship*; 10–11 Bible) and for prosperity for his people (13–16 *Common Worship*; 12–15 Bible).

It starts by praising the Lord for His protecting power. The confident, almost exuberant, first two verses use words that echo psalm 18. The glory of the Lord set out in these opening verses then prompts thoughts of the insignificance of human beings in comparison and of the brevity of human life. Verse 3 echoes psalm 8.

Then comes a prayer that uses vivid poetic metaphors to call on the Lord to take action and show His power (5–8). In grateful anticipation that the prayer will be answered, the King promises to sing a new song to the Lord (9–10).

Then comes the prayer to be rescued from

foreign armies (11–12 *Common Worship*; 11 Bible). The prayer in the final verses presents a lovely picture of a country at peace, with contented family life, fruitful fields and healthy livestock (13–15 *Common Worship*; 12–14 Bible). No wonder the psalm ends on a note of joy, with a sense of how good it is to have the Lord as our God.

• Pray for your country, that it may be protected from war, terrorism and civic violence, that it may enjoy stable family life in which children can grow up healthy and secure.

Psalm 145
A hymn of praise to the Lord of creation

They tell of the glory of your kingdom.

This hymn of praise uses a quite formal and elaborate structure as a means of expressing the praises of the Lord.

It is an acrostic, that is, each verse begins with a different letter of the Hebrew alphabet in order (except that the letter nun is left out). This helps people who try to learn it by heart.

It begins and ends with praise. Verses 1–3 and the last verse both use the words 'praise' and 'bless'.

It divides neatly into two parts, and at the centre of the psalm are three verses (11–13) which speak of the Kingdom of the Lord. The word 'kingdom' appears four times.

The Jewish rabbi Jonathan Magonet, in his book *A Rabbi Reads the Psalms*, suggests the structure of the psalm can be seen along these lines (following the Bible's verse divisions:

1–3: I *praise* and *bless* you, Lord.
4–7: People give *you* praise, Lord.
8–9: The *Lord* is merciful.
10: The faithful give *you* thanks, Lord.
11–13: Your *kingdom* is everlasting.
14–16: You provide for *all*, Lord.
17: The *Lord* is just and kind.
18–20: The Lord hears and cares for *all*.
21: All *praise and bless* the Lord.

The ordered structure of the hymn expresses the ordered and reliable world the Lord has made to provide for the creatures who live in it.

- Ponder for a while the ordered nature of the world we live in: day and night, summer and winter, springtime and harvest, and the regular supplies of food we enjoy. Thank and praise the Lord, using a few verses from the psalm or your own words.

Psalm 146
A hymn of praise to the Lord who reigns

*The Lord gives justice to those that suffer wrong
and bread to those who hunger.*

The last five psalms in the Book of Psalms are all
hymns of praise. They all begin and end with the
word 'Hallelujah', meaning 'Praise the Lord' in
Hebrew. They are sometimes called the five Hallel
psalms, from the Hebrew word for 'praise', and
sometimes they are called the Laudate psalms, from
the Latin word meaning 'praise'. The Psalter begins
with obedience but it ends with praise.

The psalm opens with praise, urging people to
put their trust in the Lord and not in any human
powers (verses 1–3 *Common Worship*; 1–4 Bible).
Then it moves into one of the finest descriptions of
the reign or Kingdom of God. The Lord gives people justice and feeds the hungry. He sets prisoners
free and protects the weak and vulnerable (5–9
Common Worship; 6–9 Bible). This is what the
world is like when the Lord reigns. These are the
values of the Kingdom of God, and the psalm ends
rejoicing that His kingdom is an enduring one for
all time.

This psalm has many similarities with Jesus' reading in the synagogue at Nazareth (Luke 4:16–19.)

It seems likely that it shaped His understanding of the Kingdom of God which was at the heart of His 'good news'.

- Pray for the groups of people mentioned in the psalm, thinking of any you have heard of recently on radio or television or in the press – for the victims of injustice, for those who go to bed hungry, for prisoners of conscience and hostages, for asylum seekers and immigrants and families without fathers.

Psalm 147
A hymn of praise to the Lord
who has brought the exiles home

*The Lord builds up Jerusalem
and gathers together the outcasts of Israel.*

Those who were deported into exile in Babylon (see the Glossary, page 48) were heartbroken at the destruction of their homes and of their lovely city of Jerusalem. Now they have come back to their homeland in joy and are rebuilding their city (verses 1–3).

The whole psalm expresses a mood of joy and gratitude. People are glad to praise the Lord. He is the one who lifts up the poor and downtrodden (6). He combines both power and tenderness. Jerusalem is called to praise Him, for His protection ('strengthening the gates') and for the peace and prosperity He gives ('the finest wheat').

The psalm emphasises the Lord's power over creation (8–10, 16–18), but it ends by focusing on revelation. Alone among the nations, He has given His word to Israel.

• Thank the Lord for those who have had to live in exile, but are now glad to be able to return home, to Chile perhaps or to Bosnia or Kosovo. Pray for them as they rebuild their lives.

Psalm 148
A hymn of praise for the whole universe to sing

Praise the Lord from the heavens ...
Praise the Lord from the earth.

This psalm calls the whole universe to praise the Lord. The psalmist delights in calling the different parts of creation – the angels; the heavenly bodies, sun, moon and stars; the earth, the sea, the weather, all plants and animals; and all human beings. All are part of the great worshipping congregation of the Lord. But the psalm ends with a reminder of His goodness to Israel, the people He has brought close to Himself.

- Think of one or two things in the creation that move you deeply, from the grandeur of a mountain range to the beauty of a tiny flower or the loveliness of a new-born kitten or puppy. Imagine them joining you in praising God.

Psalm 149
A hymn of praise for Israel to sing

Let Israel rejoice in their maker;
let the children of Zion be joyful in their king.

This psalm is something of a problem. It starts full of praise and joy, 'a new song', rejoicing in the Lord's goodness to Israel (verses 1–5). But then a negative note intrudes. These are people with 'the praises of God in their mouths and two-edged swords in their hands' (6). The Lord gives victory to the poor (4; the Hebrew word translated 'salvation' in some versions of the Bible can equally well be translated 'victory'). The defeat of powerful enemy nations which oppress weaker countries is part of the justice of God, redressing wrongs, but this psalm seems to relish executing vengeance on them. Perhaps this is the song of a weak, vulnerable nation, threatened by powerful enemies, that will only survive if it can fight them in battle and defeat them when they attack. It is a psalm that brings us down to the realities of life with a bump.

• Pray for those who have suffered great wrongs but are now in positions of power. Pray that they may be moved and guided by a clear sense of justice, and not by a desire for revenge.

Psalm 150
A hymn of praise: a doxology to end the Psalter

Let everything that has breath
praise the Lord.

This psalm is deliberately placed last in the Book of Psalms, just as psalm 1 is deliberately placed first. It is an extravagant call to praise, an uninhibited song of worship and adoration. It pictures the outcome of a life lived following the way of the Torah (Law; see the Introduction, page 28). It is an expression of the famous opening words of the Westminster Catechism: 'Man's chief end is to glorify God and to enjoy Him for ever.'

(It also tells us a good deal about the musical instruments used to accompany the singing of the psalms, and that people used to dance with tambourines as they sang.)

- Praise the Lord!